Suzy Toronto's
Wonderful Wacky Women.

The Ultimate
2020 Weekly Planner

Yes, I have all the electronic gizmos but bottom line, I'm a "write it down" kinda girl. I like having a planner that's big enough to read and small enough to shove in my purse. I couldn't find exactly what I wanted, so I decided to design my own planner. When all my friends saw it, they wanted one too. So here it is... this is it. You're holding my little brainstorm in your hand!

Welcome to my world.

Suzy

Blue Mountain Arts.
Boulder, Colorado

Survival & Sanity
Phone Numbers You Can't Afford to Lose

It's not always a good thing to trust technology. Now, don't laugh, I once accidentally dropped my cell phone into a toilet at the airport. When I reached in to retrieve it, the auto flush took it away. With no backup, I was lost. Best solution? Create a paper trail. —Suzy

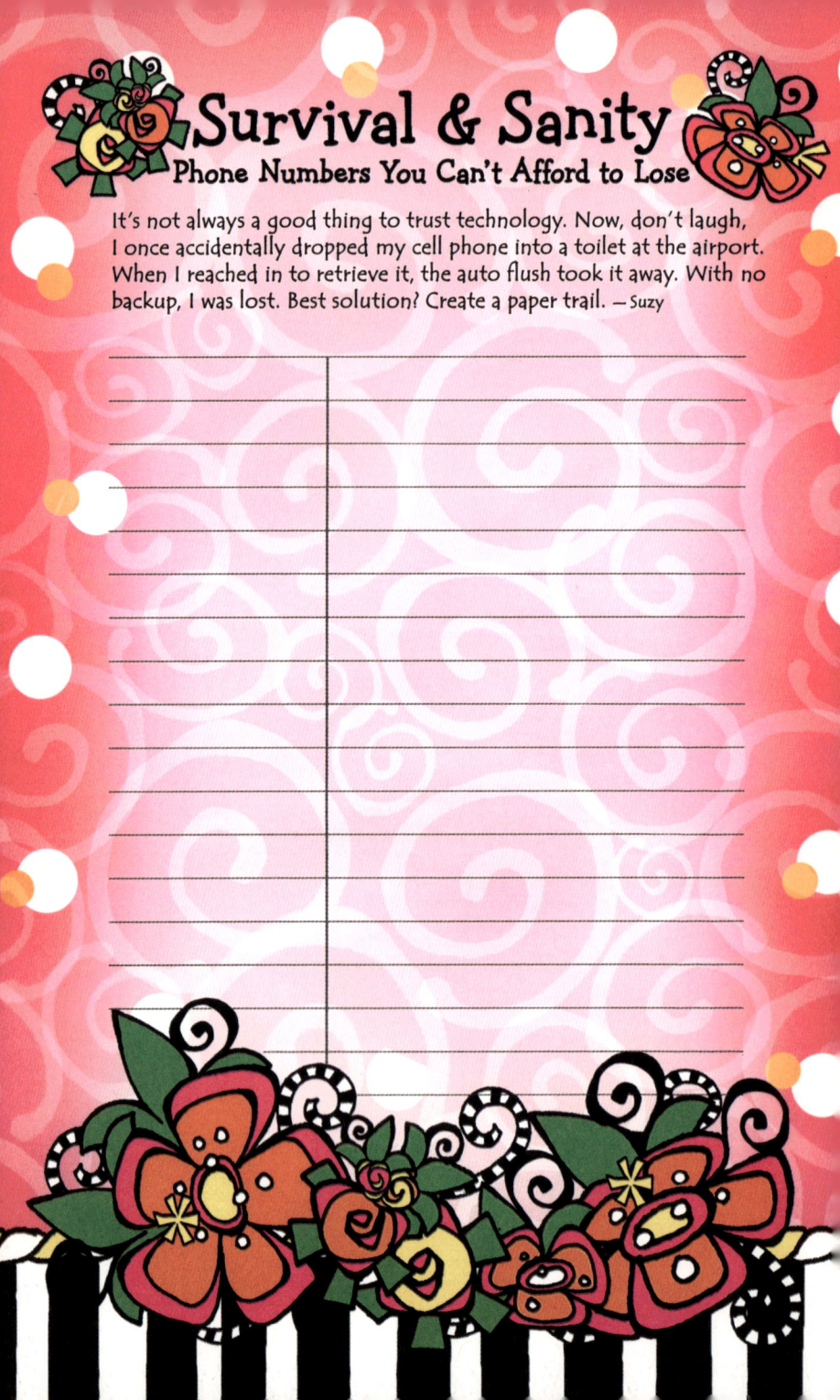

Sunday, December 29, 2019

Monday, December 30, 2019

Tuesday, December 31, 2019

New Year's Eve

Wednesday, January 1, 2020

New Year's Day

Thursday, January 2

Bank Holiday (Scotland)

Friday, January 3

Saturday, January 4

January 2020

Sunday	Monday	Tuesday	Wednesday

December 2019

S	M	T	W	T	F	S
1	2	3	4	5	6	7
8	9	10	11	12	13	14
15	16	17	18	19	20	21
22	23	24	25	26	27	28
29	30	31				

February

S	M	T	W	T	F	S
						1
2	3	4	5	6	7	8
9	10	11	12	13	14	15
16	17	18	19	20	21	22
23	24	25	26	27	28	29

1

New Year's Day

5

6

Epiphany

7

8

National Bubble Bath Day

12

13

14

15

19

20

Martin Luther King, Jr.'s
Birthday Observed (USA)

21

22

26

Australia Day (Australia)

27

28

29

Thursday	Friday	Saturday
2	3	4
9 Bank Holiday (Scotland)	10 Full Moon	11
16	17	18
23	24	25 Chinese New Year
30	31	

Notes:

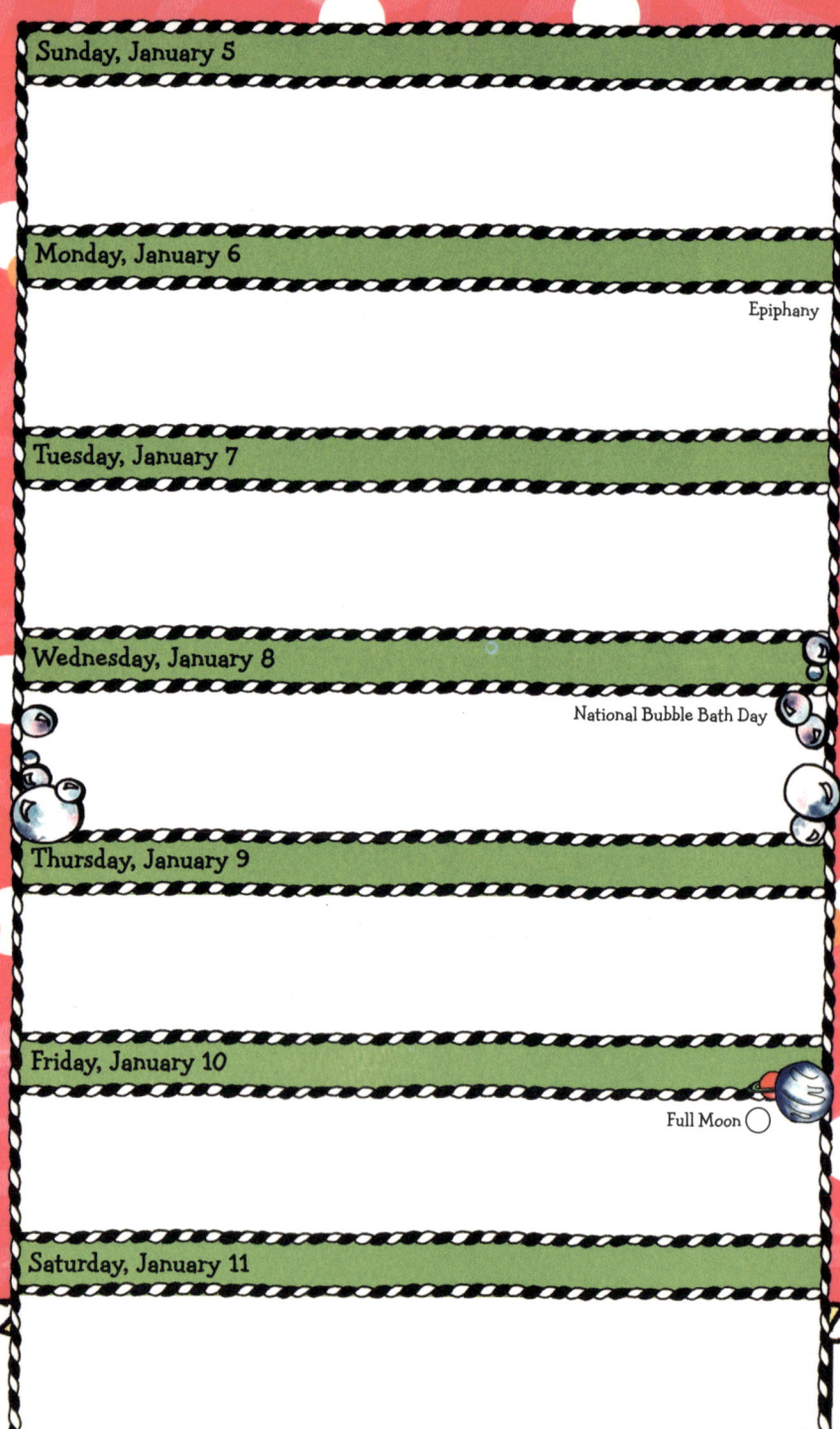

Sunday, January 5

Monday, January 6

Epiphany

Tuesday, January 7

Wednesday, January 8

National Bubble Bath Day

Thursday, January 9

Friday, January 10

Full Moon ○

Saturday, January 11

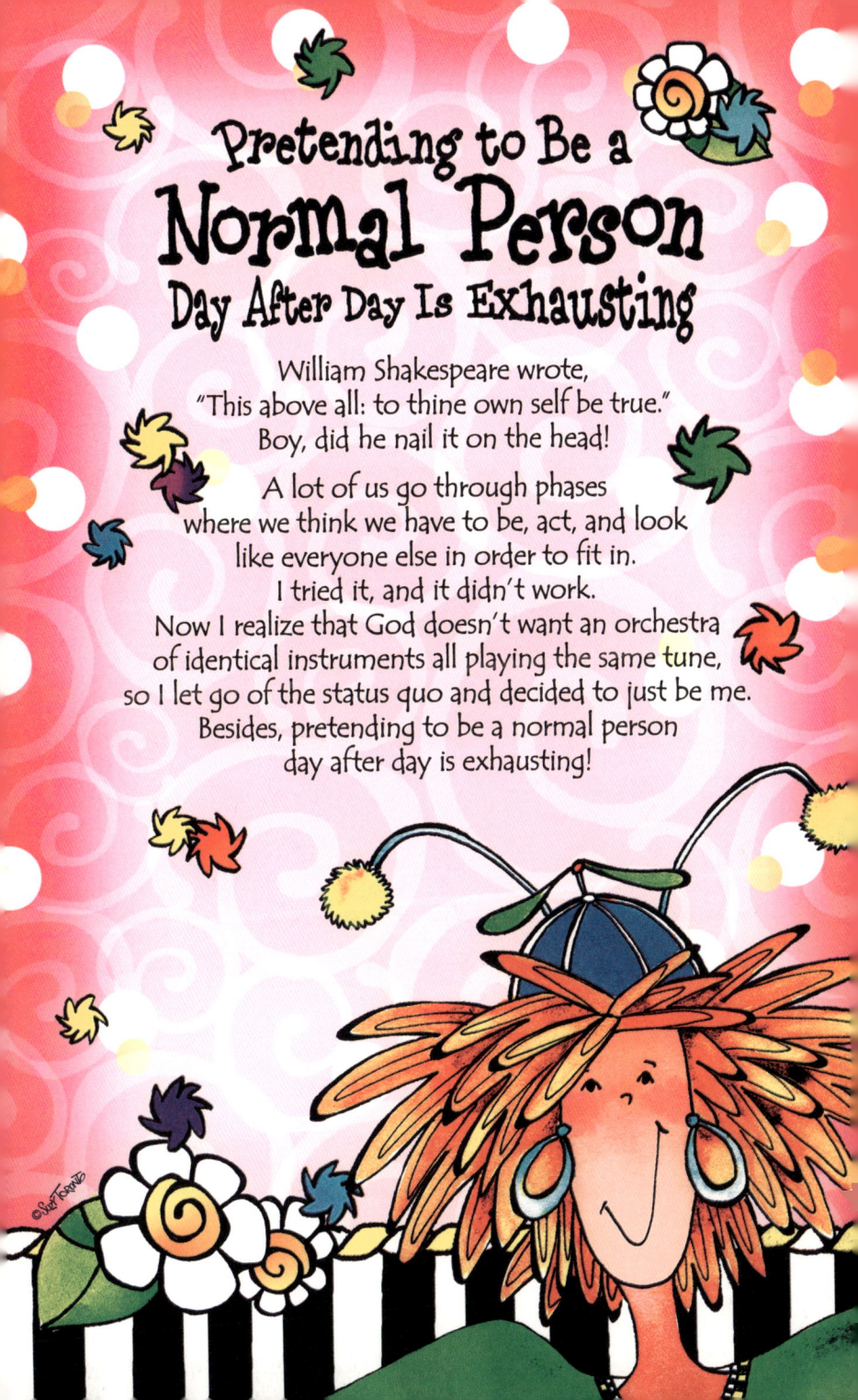

Pretending to Be a
Normal Person
Day After Day Is Exhausting

William Shakespeare wrote,
"This above all: to thine own self be true."
Boy, did he nail it on the head!

A lot of us go through phases
where we think we have to be, act, and look
like everyone else in order to fit in.
I tried it, and it didn't work.
Now I realize that God doesn't want an orchestra
of identical instruments all playing the same tune,
so I let go of the status quo and decided to just be me.
Besides, pretending to be a normal person
day after day is exhausting!

Being normal is totally overrated!

Sunday, January 12

Monday, January 13

Tuesday, January 14

Wednesday, January 15

Thursday, January 16

Friday, January 17

Saturday, January 18

Notes:

I may appear to be
a normal person
but inside I am
completely

wacky.

Sunday, January 19

Monday, January 20

Martin Luther King, Jr.'s Birthday Observed (USA)

Tuesday, January 21

Wednesday, January 22

Thursday, January 23

Friday, January 24

Saturday, January 25

Chinese New Year

When You Do Foolish Things, Do Them with Enthusiasm!

In our effort to masquerade as people who really have our acts together, goofs, blunders, and faux pas often slip out. Sometimes these missteps are so unforgettable that they start to take on a life of their own. We get our feet stuck so far in our mouths or our skirts flung up so high over our heads that the spectacle is simply hard to miss.

This is where laughing at ourselves becomes a lifesaving virtue… because when we embrace our mistakes and make the best of the situation, we can just move on.

So next time your inner "goofball" slips out, muster up all the wild energy you possess, throw your arms in the air, and give the world a cross-eyed smile!

After all, we may do foolish things… but at least we do them with enthusiasm!

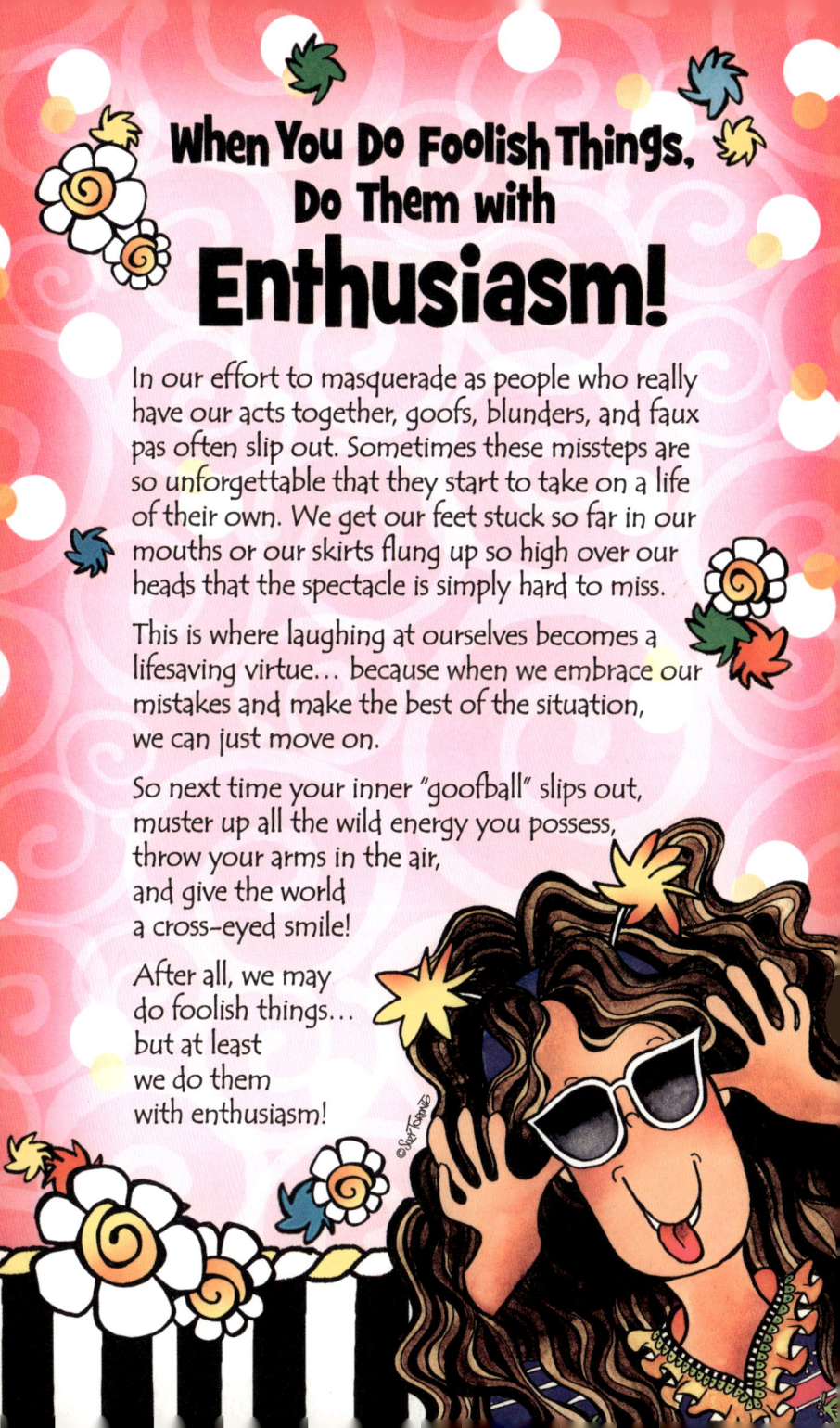

Wacky
is my superpower.

Sunday, January 26

Australia Day (Australia)

Monday, January 27

Tuesday, January 28

Wednesday, January 29

Thursday, January 30

Friday, January 31

Saturday, February 1

Black History Month Begins

Notes:

I tried being normal once.

It was the worst two minutes of my life.

February 2020

Sunday	Monday	Tuesday	Wednesday

January							March						
S	M	T	W	T	F	S	S	M	T	W	T	F	S
			1	2	3	4	1	2	3	4	5	6	7
5	6	7	8	9	10	11	8	9	10	11	12	13	14
12	13	14	15	16	17	18	15	16	17	18	19	20	21
19	20	21	22	23	24	25	22	23	24	25	26	27	28
26	27	28	29	30	31		29	30	31				

2	3	4	5
Groundhog Day			

9	10	11	12
Full Moon ◯			Lincoln's Birthday (USA)

16	17	18	19
	Presidents' Day (USA)		

23	24	25	26
		Mardi Gras Shrove Tuesday (UK)	Ash Wednesday

Thursday	Friday	Saturday
		1 Black History Month Begins
6 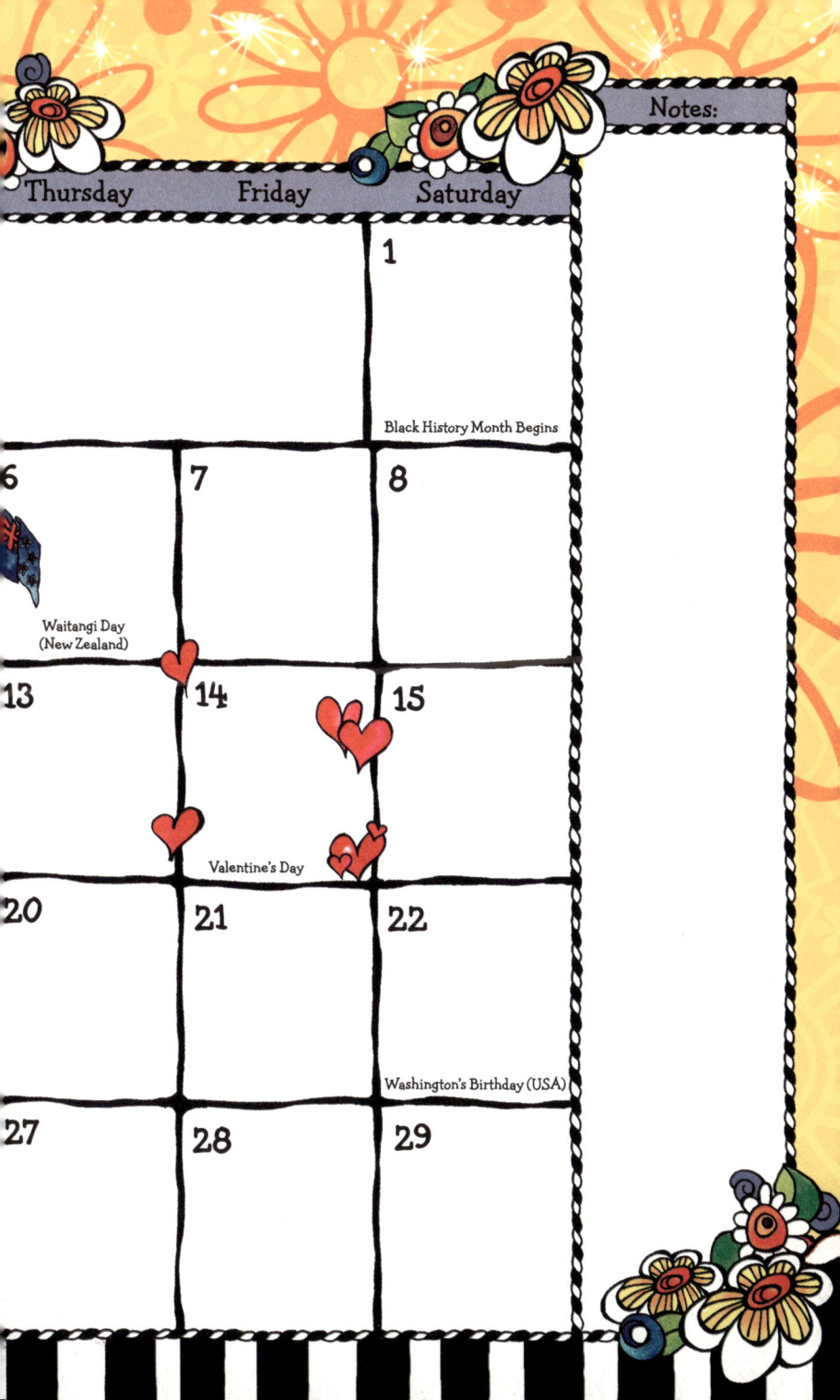 Waitangi Day (New Zealand)	**7**	**8**
13	**14** Valentine's Day	**15**
20	**21**	**22** Washington's Birthday (USA)
27	**28**	**29**

Notes:

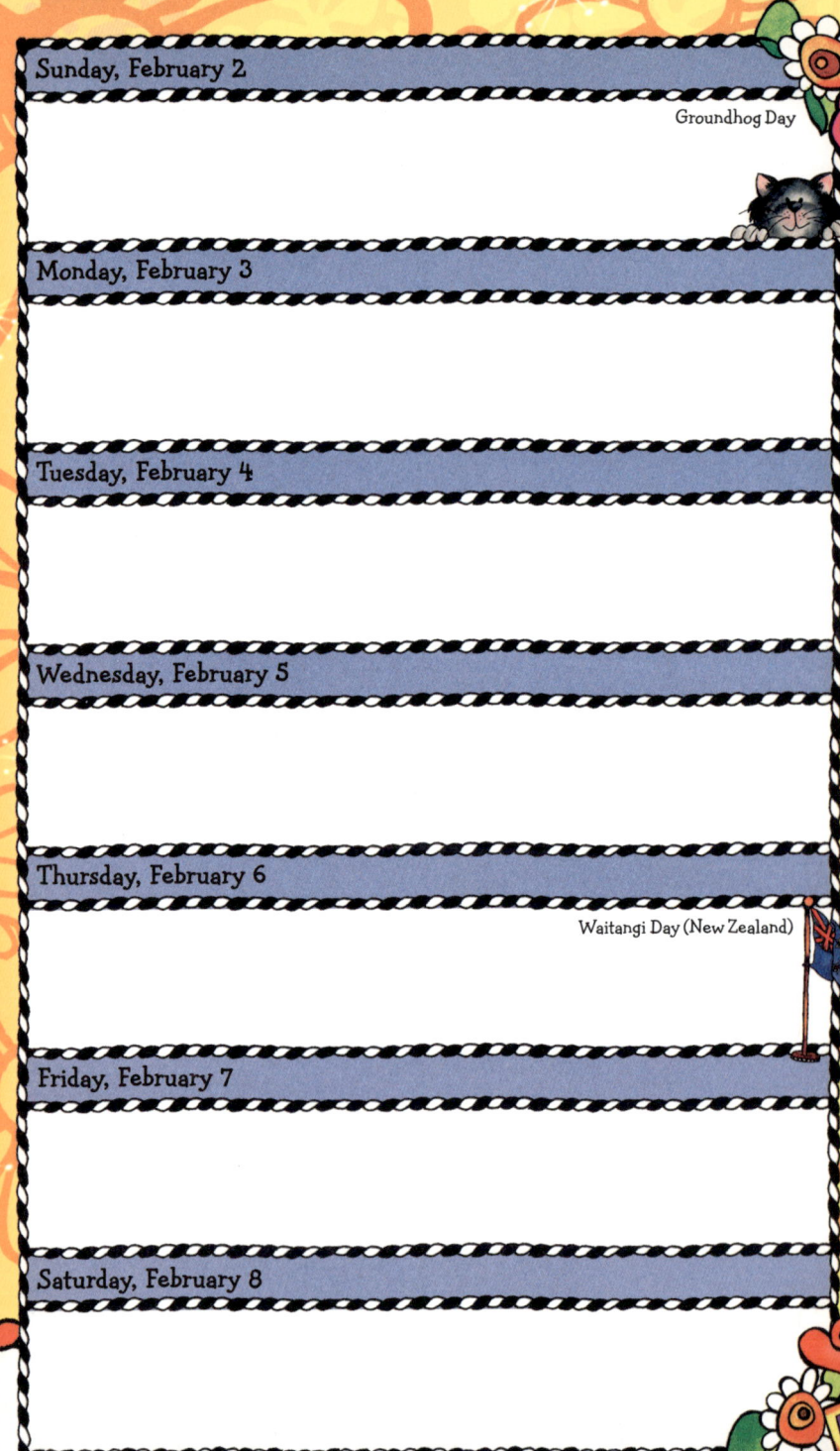

Sunday, February 2

Groundhog Day

Monday, February 3

Tuesday, February 4

Wednesday, February 5

Thursday, February 6

Waitangi Day (New Zealand)

Friday, February 7

Saturday, February 8

Art DOES NOT HAVE TO MATCH YOUR SOFA

I want to know where it says,
"The art you put in your home has to match your sofa."

First of all, art is not meant
to decorate your home…
art is meant to decorate your soul.
It is the signature of every civilization
that ever left its mark on earth.
It breaks all the rules and shakes off
the dust of everyday life.

With a power like that,
who cares if it matches your sofa?
Let it match your soul!

©Suzy Toronto

Every artist was once an amateur.

Sunday, February 9

Full Moon ○

Monday, February 10

Tuesday, February 11

Wednesday, February 12

Lincoln's Birthday (USA)

Thursday, February 13

Friday, February 14

Valentine's Day

Saturday, February 15

Notes:

Let your creativity
run wild.
Express yourself
in art.

Sunday, February 16

Monday, February 17

Presidents' Day (USA)

Tuesday, February 18

Wednesday, February 19

Thursday, February 20

Friday, February 21

Saturday, February 22

Washington's Birthday (USA)

The Art of Doing Nothing

Do you know what talented, high-energy people
do when they need a break? They do nothing!
I'm not saying they don't take time off
or go on vacation… they most certainly do!
But instead of running around at 90 mph
trying to do and see everything, they concentrate
on *not* doing anything at all. It's not about being lazy.
It's about taking the time to breathe… zoning out
to zero for a few days and stepping back from normal life
to regroup. It takes years to master, but once you
perfect it, you'll realize how wonderful it is.
With both body and spirit renewed
you'll agree it is time well spent.
So give "doing nothing" a try.
I think you're going to be
really great at it!

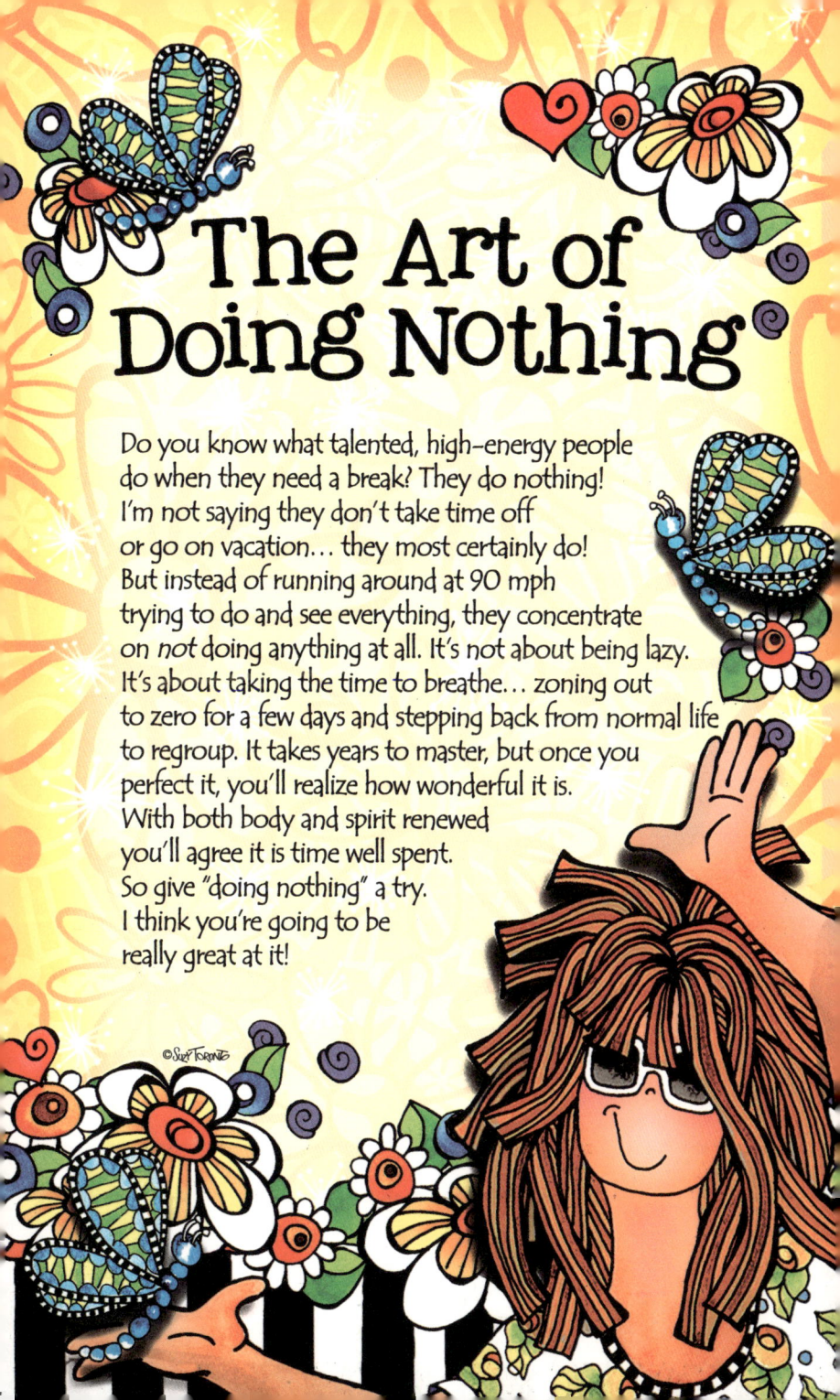

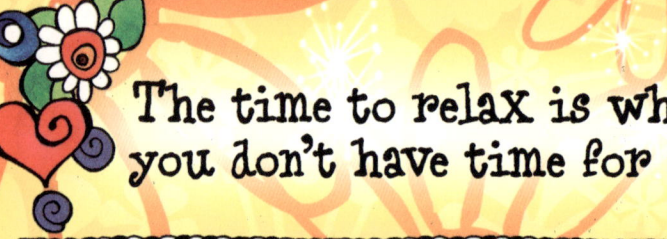

The time to relax is when you don't have time for it.

Sunday, February 23

Monday, February 24

Tuesday, February 25

Mardi Gras
Shrove Tuesday (UK)

Wednesday, February 26

Ash Wednesday

Thursday, February 27

Friday, February 28

Saturday, February 29

Notes:

Sometimes the most productive thing to do is just *Relax.*

March 2020

Sunday	Monday	Tuesday	Wednesday
1 National Women's History Month Begins (USA) St. David's Day (Wales)	**2**	**3**	**4**
8 International Women's Day Girl Scout Week Begins (USA) USA/Canada Daylight Saving Time Begins	**9** Commonwealth Day (UK) Full Moon	**10** Purim	**11**
15	**16**	**17** St. Patrick's Day	**18**
22 Mothering Sunday (UK)	**23**	**24**	**25**
29 UK/Ireland Daylight Saving Time Begins	**30**	**31**	

Thursday	Friday	Saturday
5	6	7
12	13	14
19	20 Spring Begins	21 Human Rights Day (South Africa)
26	27	28

Notes:

February						
S	M	T	W	T	F	S
						1
2	3	4	5	6	7	8
9	10	11	12	13	14	15
16	17	18	19	20	21	22
23	24	25	26	27	28	29

April						
S	M	T	W	T	F	S
		1	2	3	4
5	6	7	8	9	10	11
12	13	14	15	16	17	18
19	20	21	22	23	24	25
26	27	28	29	30		

Sunday, March 1

National Women's History Month Begins (USA)
St. David's Day (Wales)

Monday, March 2

Tuesday, March 3

Wednesday, March 4

Thursday, March 5

Friday, March 6

Saturday, March 7

Plan B

Plan A is always my first choice.
You know, the one where everything
works out to be happily ever after.

But more often than not, I find myself dealing
with the upside-down, inside-out version
where nothing goes as it should. It's at this point
the real test of my character comes in…
Do I sink or do I swim? Do I wallow in self-pity
and play the victim or simply shift gears
and make the best of the situation?

The choice is mine. After all…
life is all about how you handle Plan B.

©Suzy Toronto

Embrace new possibilities!

Sunday, March 8

International Women's Day
Girl Scout Week Begins (USA)
USA/Canada Daylight Saving Time Begins

Monday, March 9

Commonwealth Day (UK)
Full Moon ○

Tuesday, March 10

Purim

Wednesday, March 11

Thursday, March 12

Friday, March 13

Saturday, March 14

Notes:

Circumstances
do not define us.

But how we cope
with them does.

Sunday, March 15

Monday, March 16

Tuesday, March 17

St. Patrick's Day

Wednesday, March 18

Thursday, March 19

Friday, March 20

Spring Begins

Saturday, March 21

Human Rights Day (South Africa)

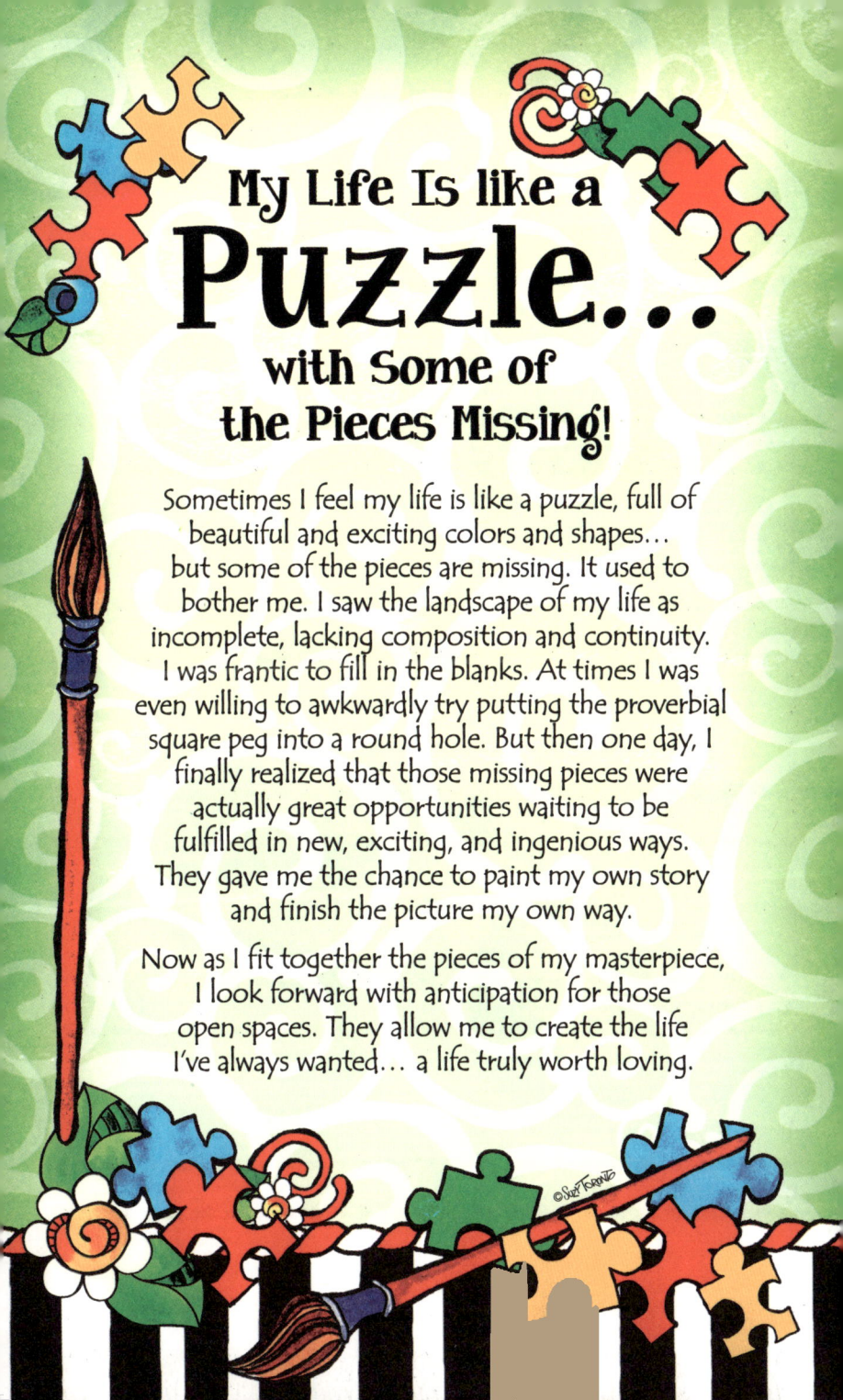

My Life Is like a
Puzzle...
with Some of
the Pieces Missing!

Sometimes I feel my life is like a puzzle, full of
beautiful and exciting colors and shapes…
but some of the pieces are missing. It used to
bother me. I saw the landscape of my life as
incomplete, lacking composition and continuity.
I was frantic to fill in the blanks. At times I was
even willing to awkwardly try putting the proverbial
square peg into a round hole. But then one day, I
finally realized that those missing pieces were
actually great opportunities waiting to be
fulfilled in new, exciting, and ingenious ways.
They gave me the chance to paint my own story
and finish the picture my own way.

Now as I fit together the pieces of my masterpiece,
I look forward with anticipation for those
open spaces. They allow me to create the life
I've always wanted… a life truly worth loving.

©Suzy Toronto

Sunday, March 22

Mothering Sunday (UK)

Monday, March 23

Tuesday, March 24

Wednesday, March 25

Thursday, March 26

Friday, March 27

Saturday, March 28

Sunday, March 29

UK/Ireland Daylight Saving Time Begins

Monday, March 30

Tuesday, March 31

Wednesday, April 1

April Fools' Day

Thursday, April 2

Friday, April 3

Saturday, April 4

April 2020

Sunday	Monday	Tuesday	Wednesday
March

S M T W T F S
1 2 3 4 5 6 7
8 9 10 11 12 13 14
15 16 17 18 19 20 21
22 23 24 25 26 27 28
29 30 31 | May

S M T W T F S
1 2
3 4 5 6 7 8 9
10 11 12 13 14 15 16
17 18 19 20 21 22 23
24/31 25 26 27 28 29 30 | | **1**

April Fools' Day |
| **5**

Palm Sunday | **6** | **7**

Full Moon ○ | **8** |
| **12**

Easter Sunday | **13**

Easter Monday (Canada/ UK/Ireland/Australia) Family Day (South Africa) | **14**

Reach as High as You Can Day | **15** |
| **19**

Orthodox Easter Sunday | **20** | **21**

Holocaust Remembrance Day (Yom Hashoah) | **22**

Administrative Professionals Day Earth Day |
| **26** | **27**

Freedom Day (South Africa) | **28** | **29** |

Thursday	Friday	Saturday
2	3	4
9 First Day of Passover	10 Good Friday	11
16	17	18
23 Take Our Daughters and Sons to Work Day (USA) St. George's Day (UK)	24 First Day of Ramadan	25 ANZAC Day (Australia/New Zealand)
30		

Notes:

Sunday, April 5

Palm Sunday

Monday, April 6

Tuesday, April 7

Full Moon ◯

Wednesday, April 8

Thursday, April 9

First Day of Passover

Friday, April 10

Good Friday

Saturday, April 11

In a World Where You Can Be Anything... Be Kind

"What are you going to be when you grow up?" Most of us remember being asked that question as a kid. As we grew older, that simple question was expanded to the adult version: "So, what do you do?"

But the answer to this perpetual question doesn't magically tell the inquirer *everything* they need to know about us. Although a career may well define our passions or interests, it doesn't reveal much about who we really are. What if the next time someone asked "What do you do?", instead of answering by way of a profession or title, we simply said "I try to be kind to everyone I meet."

In a world where we really can be anything our hearts desire, why don't we strive to put virtues on the top of our list? Qualities like integrity, charity, honor, and simple kindness have the power to change lives on a scale never before achieved and carve a lasting impression into the human experience. They not only uplift those we encounter, but are in fact steppingstones on the path that leads us toward truly living a life worth loving!

©Suzy Toronto

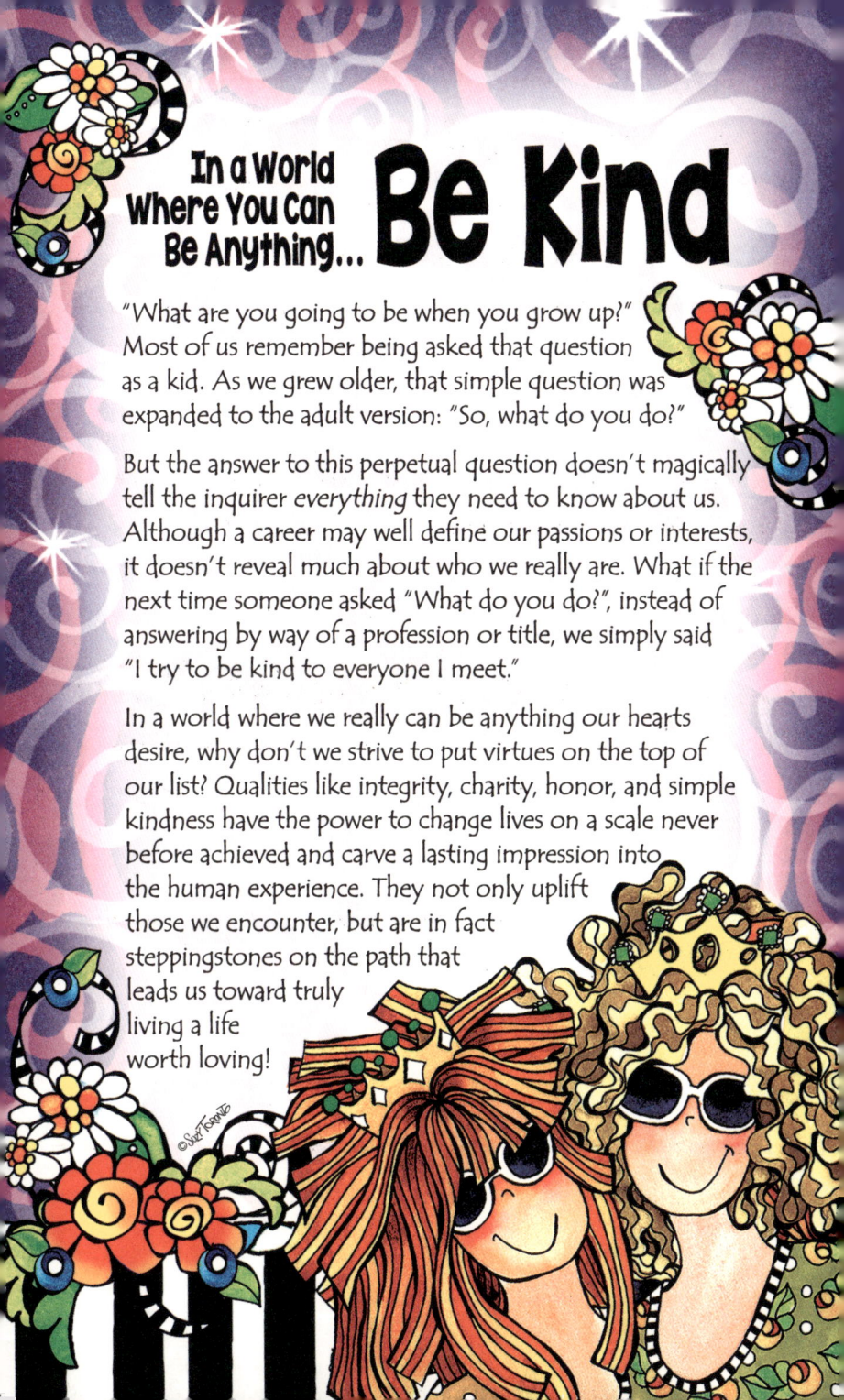

Always be a hug waiting to happen.

Sunday, April 12

Easter Sunday

Monday, April 13

Easter Monday (Canada/UK/Ireland/Australia)
Family Day (South Africa)

Tuesday, April 14

Reach as High as You Can Day

Wednesday, April 15

Thursday, April 16

Friday, April 17

Saturday, April 18

Notes:

You will never regret being too Kind.

Sunday, April 19

Orthodox Easter Sunday

Monday, April 20

Tuesday, April 21

Holocaust Remembrance Day (Yom Hashoah)

Wednesday, April 22

Administrative Professionals Day
Earth Day

Thursday, April 23

Take Our Daughters and Sons to Work Day (USA)
St. George's Day (UK)

Friday, April 24

First Day of Ramadan

Saturday, April 25

ANZAC Day (Australia/New Zealand)

Always Color OUTSIDE the Lines

As a child I was taught
to always paint the sky blue
and the grass green. I was told to be very careful
and try to stay inside the lines.

Why did they do that? Life is too full of possibilities
to conform to unimportant rules that in the end
don't matter. Rules like these stifle our creativity and
halt our progress toward achieving our full potential.

So let them go. Discard those dictates that
defined your old parameters and reach
for the colors you've never tried.
Splash violet, melon, and
chartreuse all over your work...
and splatter it on the floor if
the spirit so moves you.
For now is the time to
embrace your creativity.
Break the rules...
and whatever you do,
don't worry about
staying inside the lines.

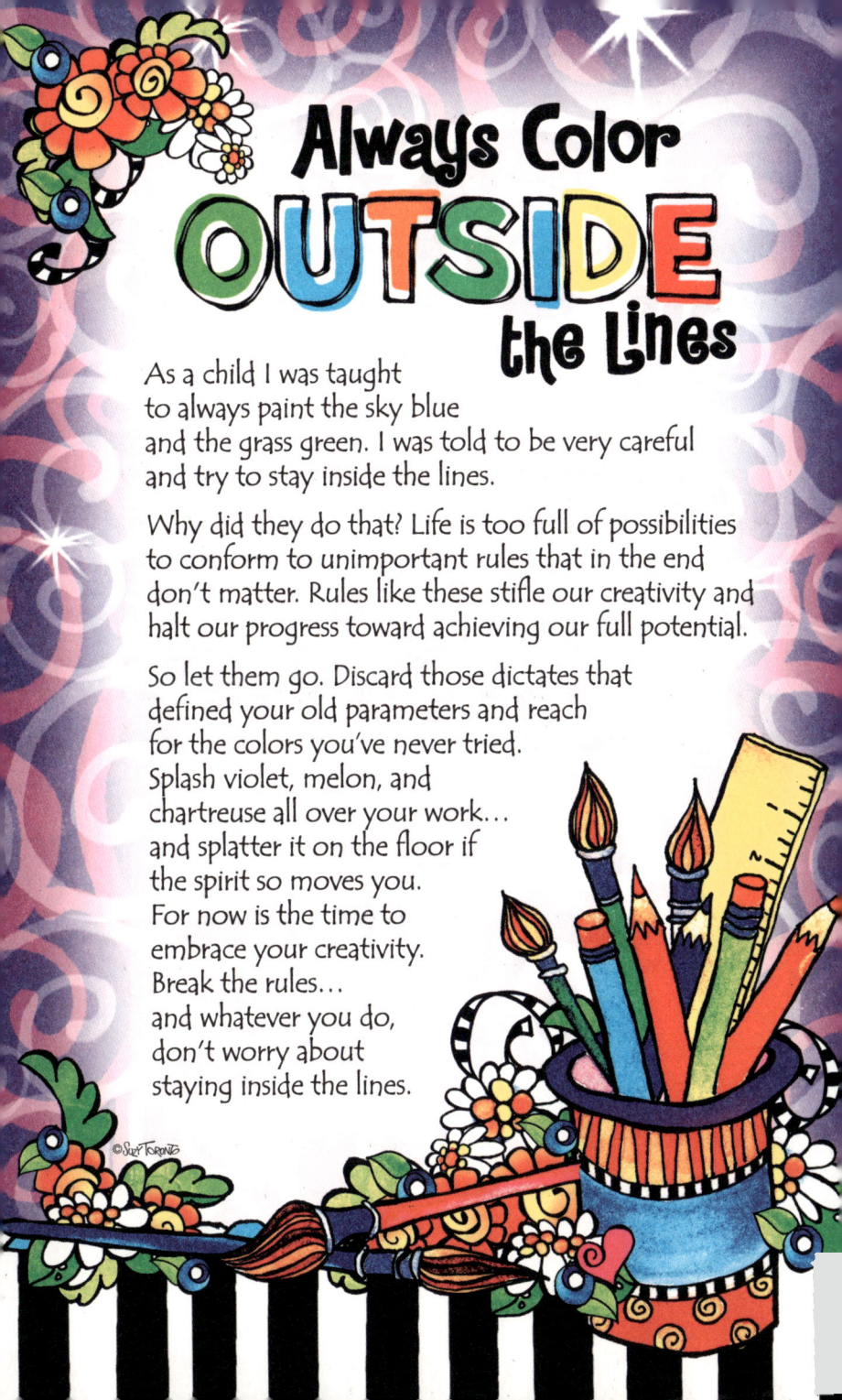

Creative minds inspire others.

Sunday, April 26

Monday, April 27

Freedom Day (South Africa)

Tuesday, April 28

Wednesday, April 29

Thursday, April 30

Friday, May 1

May Day
Workers' Day (South Africa)

Saturday, May 2

Notes:

Don't try to
think outside
the box.

Get rid of
the box!

May 2020

Sunday	Monday	Tuesday	Wednesday

April
S	M	T	W	T	F	S
				1	2	3	4
5	6	7	8	9	10	11
12	13	14	15	16	17	18
19	20	21	22	23	24	25
26	27	28	29	30		

June
S	M	T	W	T	F	S
	1	2	3	4	5	6
7	8	9	10	11	12	13
14	15	16	17	18	19	20
21	22	23	24	25	26	27
28	29	30				

3	4	5	6
	Bank Holiday (UK/Ireland)	National Teacher Day (USA) Cinco de Mayo	
10	11	12	13
Mother's Day			
17	18	19	20
	Victoria Day (Canada)		
24 Eid al-Fitr	25	26	27
Pentecost 31	Memorial Day Observed (USA) Bank Holiday (UK)		

Thursday	Friday	Saturday
	1	2
	May Day Workers' Day (South Africa)	
7	8	9
Full Moon ○		Lost Sock Memorial Day
14	15	16
		Armed Forces Day (USA)
21	22	23
28	29	30
	First Day of Shavuot	

Notes:

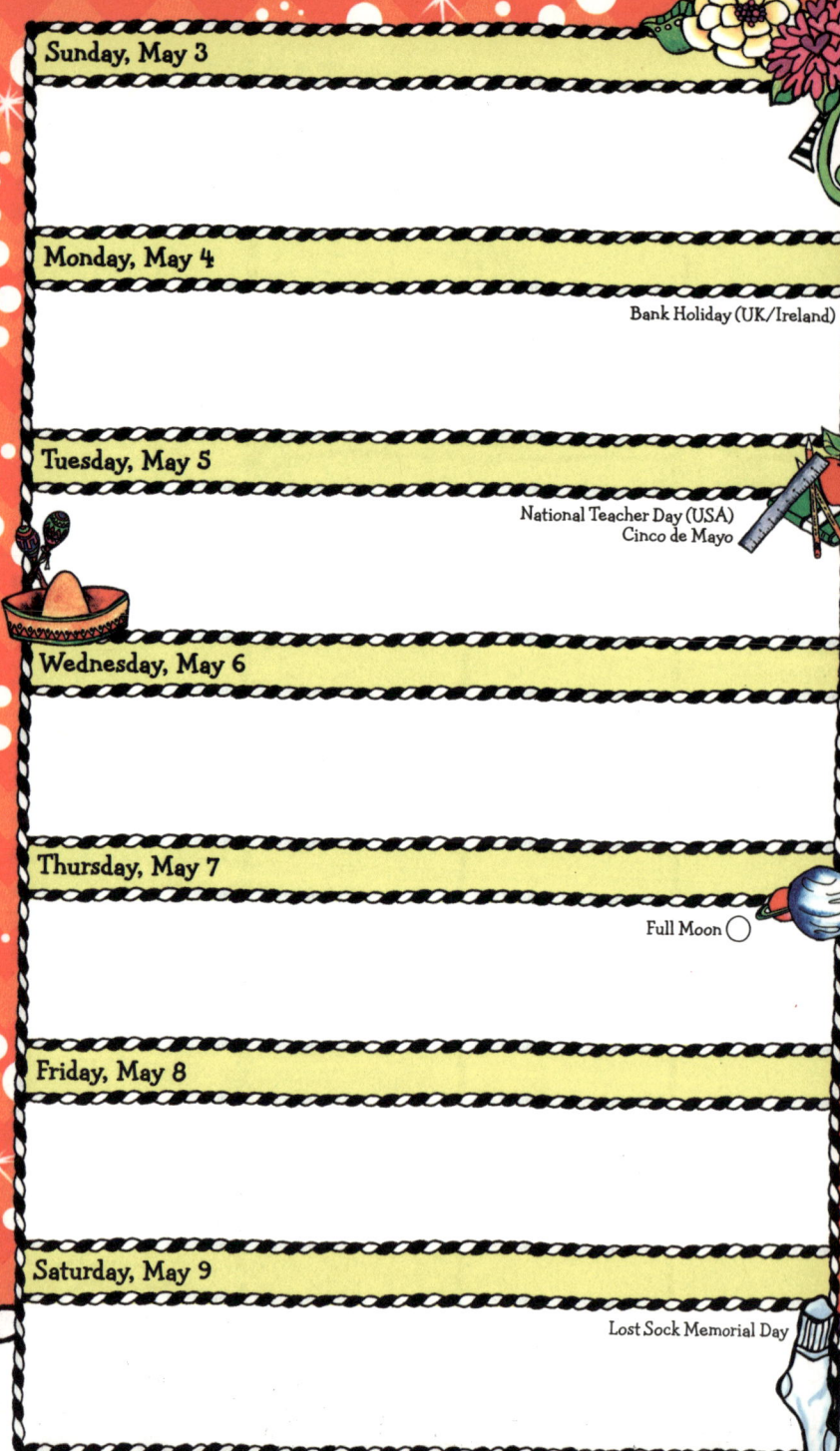

Sunday, May 3

Monday, May 4

Bank Holiday (UK/Ireland)

Tuesday, May 5

National Teacher Day (USA)
Cinco de Mayo

Wednesday, May 6

Thursday, May 7

Full Moon ○

Friday, May 8

Saturday, May 9

Lost Sock Memorial Day

When Life Becomes a
Roller Coaster,
Climb into the Front Seat,
Throw Your Arms in the Air,
& Enjoy the Ride!

Life is full of ups and downs. If you're anything like me, more than once you've prayed to God to take away some of the low spots. If I had only realized that the experience I was trying to avoid was actually a life-altering opportunity that shaped me into the woman I am today, I would have yelled, "Hit me with your best shot!"

Knowing this after the fact didn't make it any easier, but I now realize I'm a better person for having endured it. I learned that in the future I will try to face those challenges head-on with grace, style, and conviction.

So the next time your life starts to resemble a roller coaster, climb into the front seat, throw your arms in the air, and enjoy the ride!

©Suzy Toronto

Let the adventure begin.

Sunday, May 10

Mother's Day

Monday, May 11

Tuesday, May 12

Wednesday, May 13

Thursday, May 14

Friday, May 15

Saturday, May 16

Armed Forces Day (USA)

Notes:

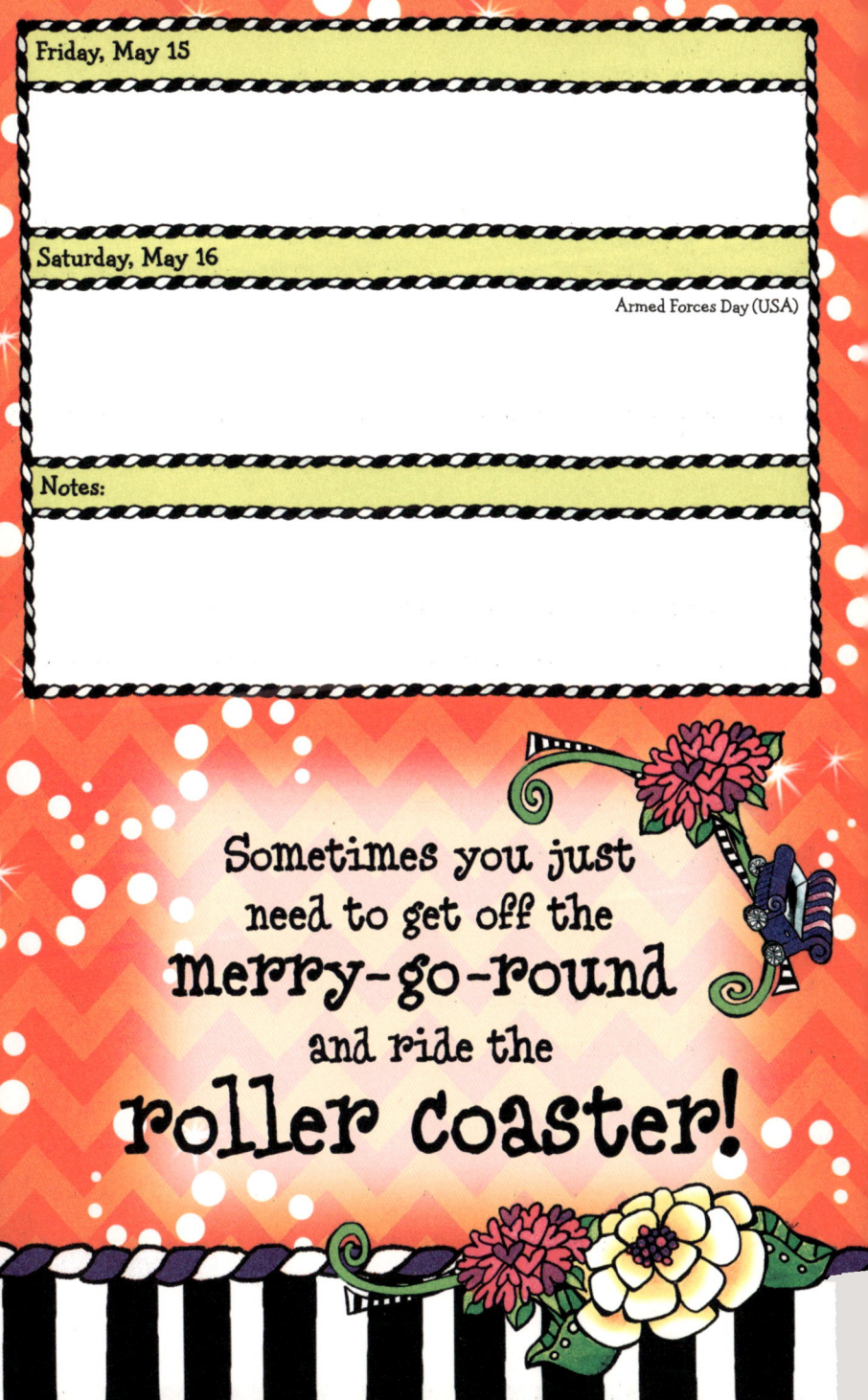

Sometimes you just
need to get off the
merry-go-round
and ride the
roller coaster!

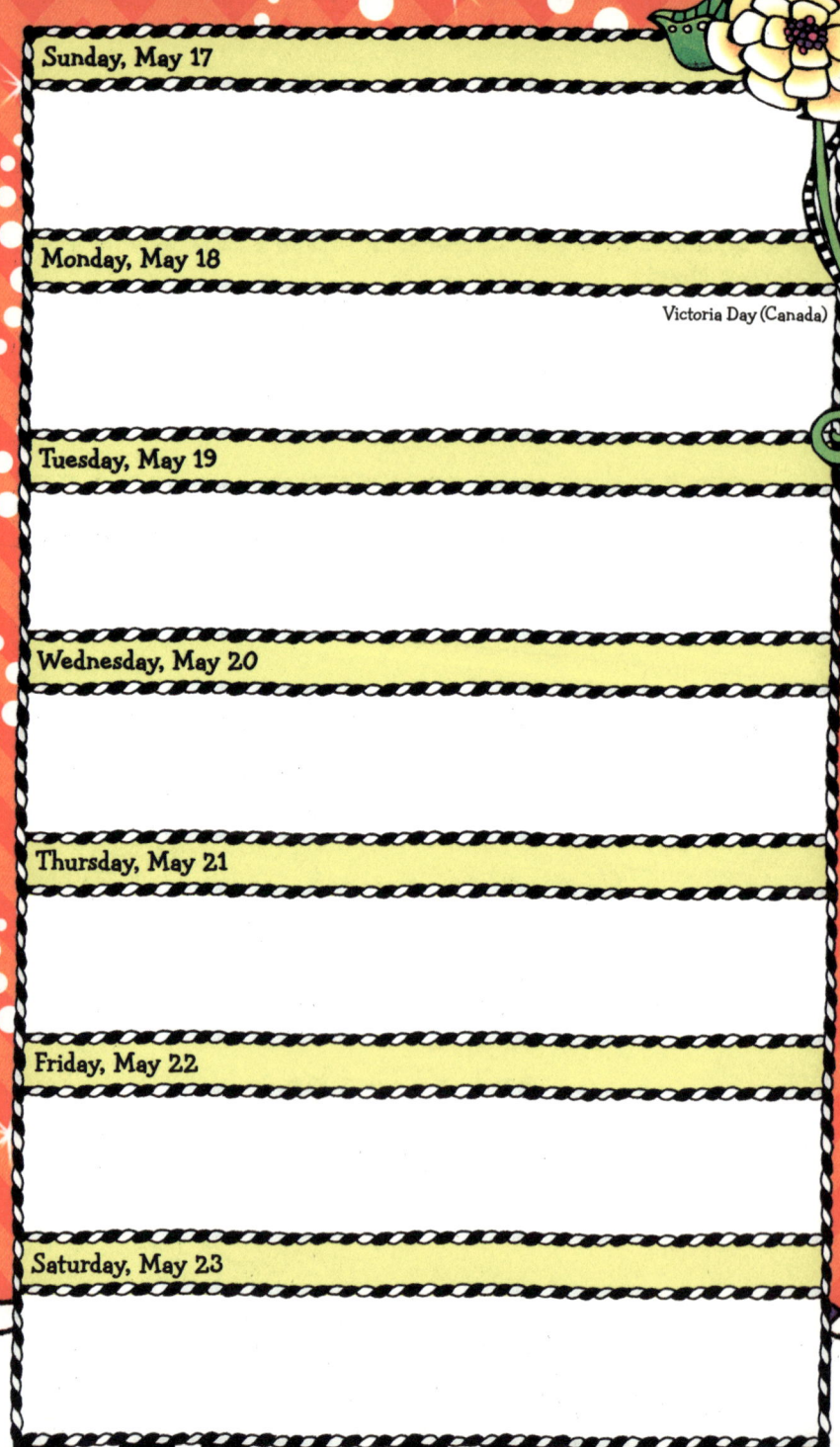

Sunday, May 17

Monday, May 18

Victoria Day (Canada)

Tuesday, May 19

Wednesday, May 20

Thursday, May 21

Friday, May 22

Saturday, May 23

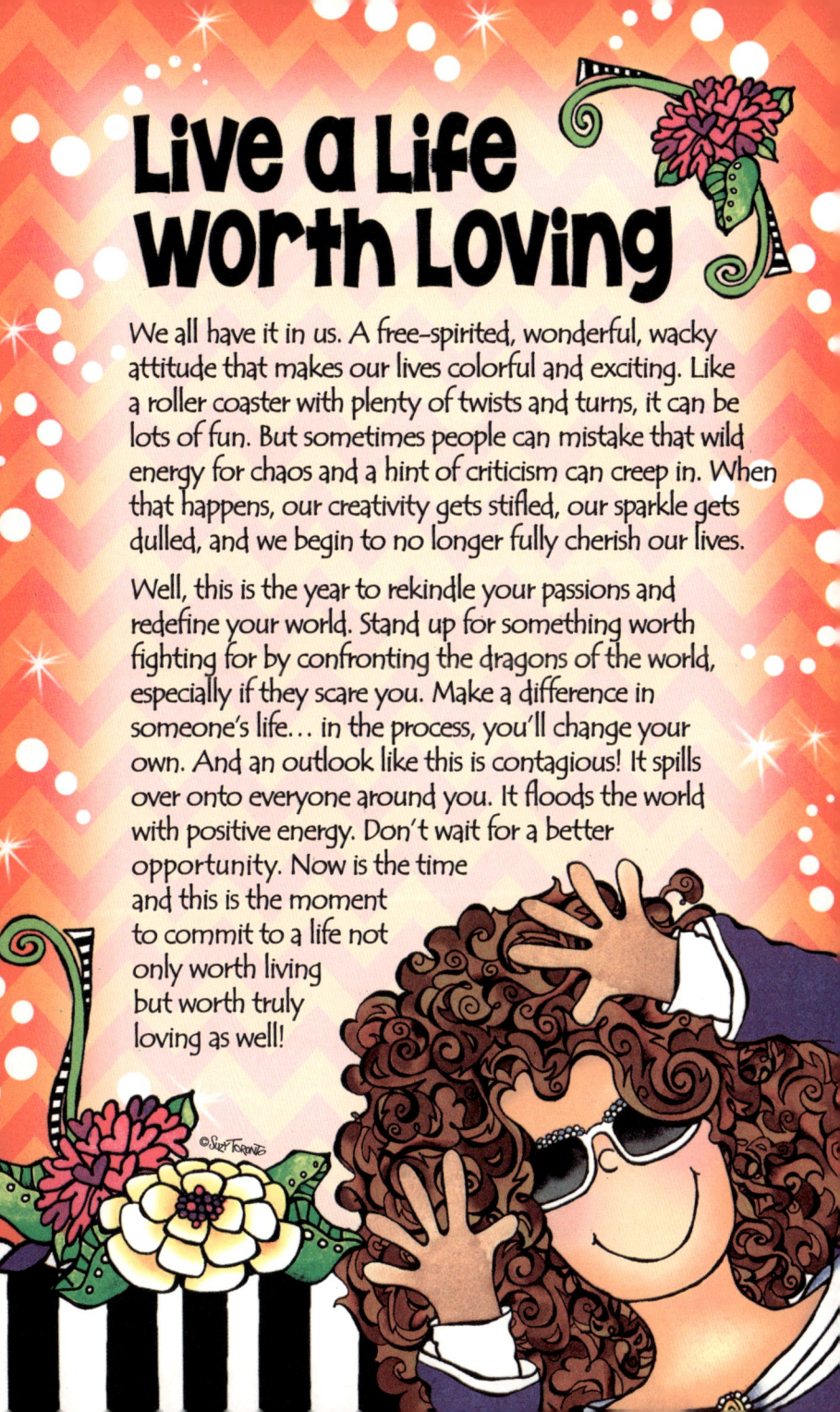

Live a Life worth Loving

We all have it in us. A free-spirited, wonderful, wacky attitude that makes our lives colorful and exciting. Like a roller coaster with plenty of twists and turns, it can be lots of fun. But sometimes people can mistake that wild energy for chaos and a hint of criticism can creep in. When that happens, our creativity gets stifled, our sparkle gets dulled, and we begin to no longer fully cherish our lives.

Well, this is the year to rekindle your passions and redefine your world. Stand up for something worth fighting for by confronting the dragons of the world, especially if they scare you. Make a difference in someone's life… in the process, you'll change your own. And an outlook like this is contagious! It spills over onto everyone around you. It floods the world with positive energy. Don't wait for a better opportunity. Now is the time and this is the moment to commit to a life not only worth living but worth truly loving as well!

Sunday, May 24

Eid al-Fitr

Monday, May 25

Memorial Day Observed (USA)
Bank Holiday (UK)

Tuesday, May 26

Wednesday, May 27

Thursday, May 28

Friday, May 29

First Day of Shavuot

Saturday, May 30

Sunday, May 31

Pentecost

Monday, June 1

National Go Barefoot Day
Bank Holiday (Ireland)

Tuesday, June 2

Wednesday, June 3

Thursday, June 4

Hug Your Cat Day

Friday, June 5

Full Moon ◯

Saturday, June 6

June 2020

Sunday	Monday	Tuesday	Wednesday
	1  National Go Barefoot Day Bank Holiday (Ireland)	**2**	**3**
7	**8**	**9**	**10**
14 Flag Day (USA)	**15**	**16** Youth Day (South Africa)	**17**
21 Father's Day	**22**	**23**	**24** St. Jean Baptiste Day (Québec)
28	**29**	**30**	

Thursday	Friday	Saturday	Notes:
4 Hug Your Cat Day	5 Full Moon ○	6	
11	12	13 Queen's Birthday (UK)	
18	19	20 Summer Begins	
25	26	27	

May						
S	M	T	W	T	F	S
					1	2
3	4	5	6	7	8	9
10	11	12	13	14	15	16
17	18	19	20	21	22	23
24/31	25	26	27	28	29	30

July						
S	M	T	W	T	F	S
			1	2	3	4
5	6	7	8	9	10	11
12	13	14	15	16	17	18
19	20	21	22	23	24	25
26	27	28	29	30	31	

Sunday, June 7

Monday, June 8

Tuesday, June 9

Wednesday, June 10

Thursday, June 11

Friday, June 12

Saturday, June 13

Queen's Birthday (UK)

Rise by Lifting Others

(No Hot Air Required!)

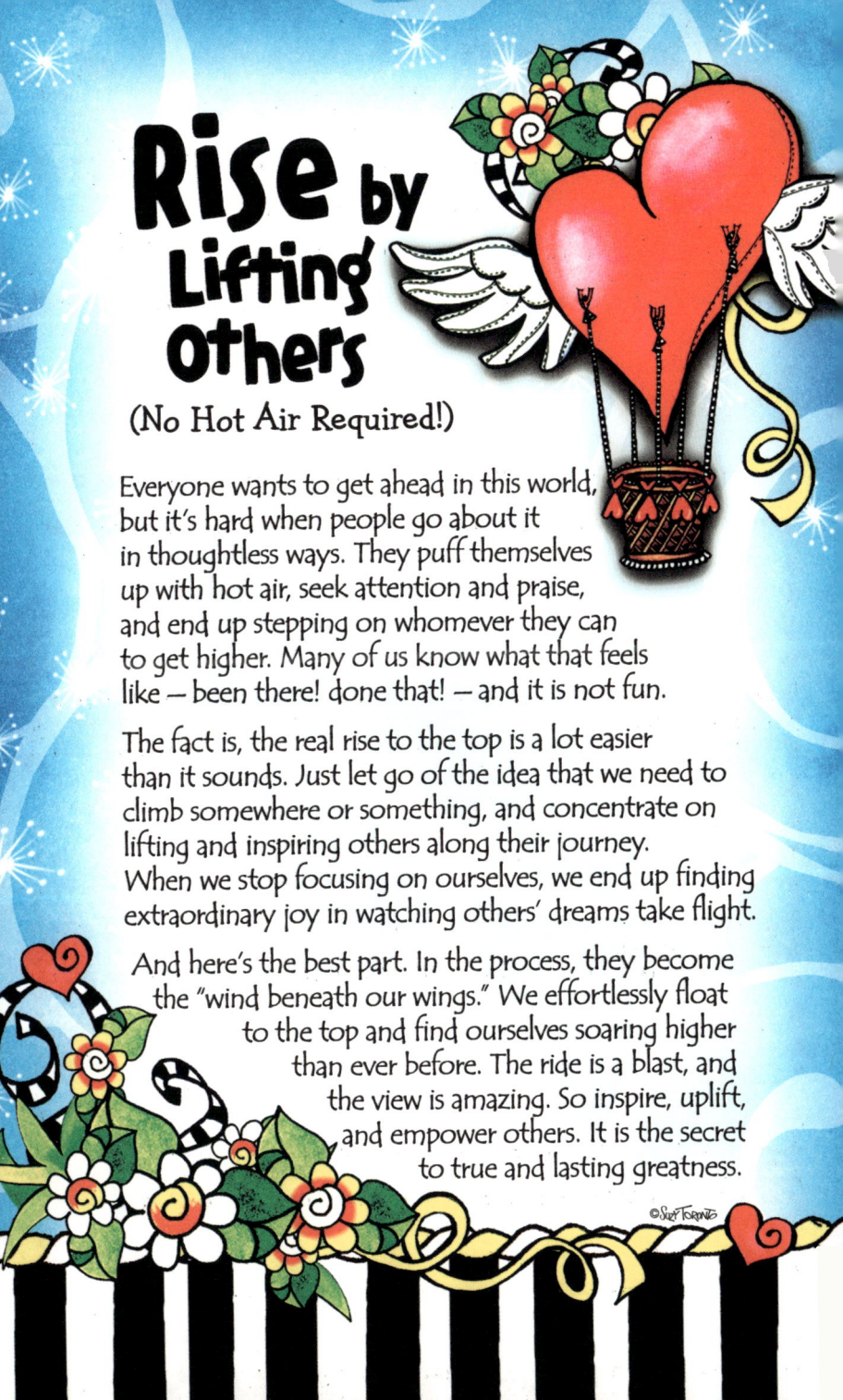

Everyone wants to get ahead in this world, but it's hard when people go about it in thoughtless ways. They puff themselves up with hot air, seek attention and praise, and end up stepping on whomever they can to get higher. Many of us know what that feels like — been there! done that! — and it is not fun.

The fact is, the real rise to the top is a lot easier than it sounds. Just let go of the idea that we need to climb somewhere or something, and concentrate on lifting and inspiring others along their journey. When we stop focusing on ourselves, we end up finding extraordinary joy in watching others' dreams take flight.

And here's the best part. In the process, they become the "wind beneath our wings." We effortlessly float to the top and find ourselves soaring higher than ever before. The ride is a blast, and the view is amazing. So inspire, uplift, and empower others. It is the secret to true and lasting greatness.

©Suzy Toronto

If you're too busy to **serve others,** you're too busy.

Sunday, June 14

Flag Day (USA)

Monday, June 15

Tuesday, June 16

Youth Day (South Africa)

Wednesday, June 17

Thursday, June 18

Friday, June 19

Saturday, June 20

Summer Begins

Notes:

The happiest people I know
are the ones who
lose themselves
in service.

Sunday, June 21

Father's Day

Monday, June 22

Tuesday, June 23

Wednesday, June 24

St. Jean Baptiste Day (Québec)

Thursday, June 25

Friday, June 26

Saturday, June 27

BECOMING AN ADULT IS
the Dumbest Thing
I Ever Did

Like most young people, I couldn't wait to come of age and be a real certified grownup. Impatiently I waited for my birthday so I could declare to the world that I was officially an adult! But now I wonder why I was in such a hurry. In retrospect, becoming an adult is the dumbest thing I ever did.

The truth is, growing old is mandatory — but growing up is not. In fact, I think it's a trap to be avoided at all costs!

And since being an adult is just not working for me, I've decided that maybe, just maybe, it's not too late. From now on I'm going to stop ignoring my inner child and embrace all things "kid." I'm going to live, love, and play with the wild passion and spontaneity we all once had. So be warned — the kid in me is coming out! And if you happen to feel the urge to give me milk and cookies, wipe my face, and put me down for a nap, go ahead. 'Cause when it comes to childhood, I'm hitting the do-over button! Wanna play?

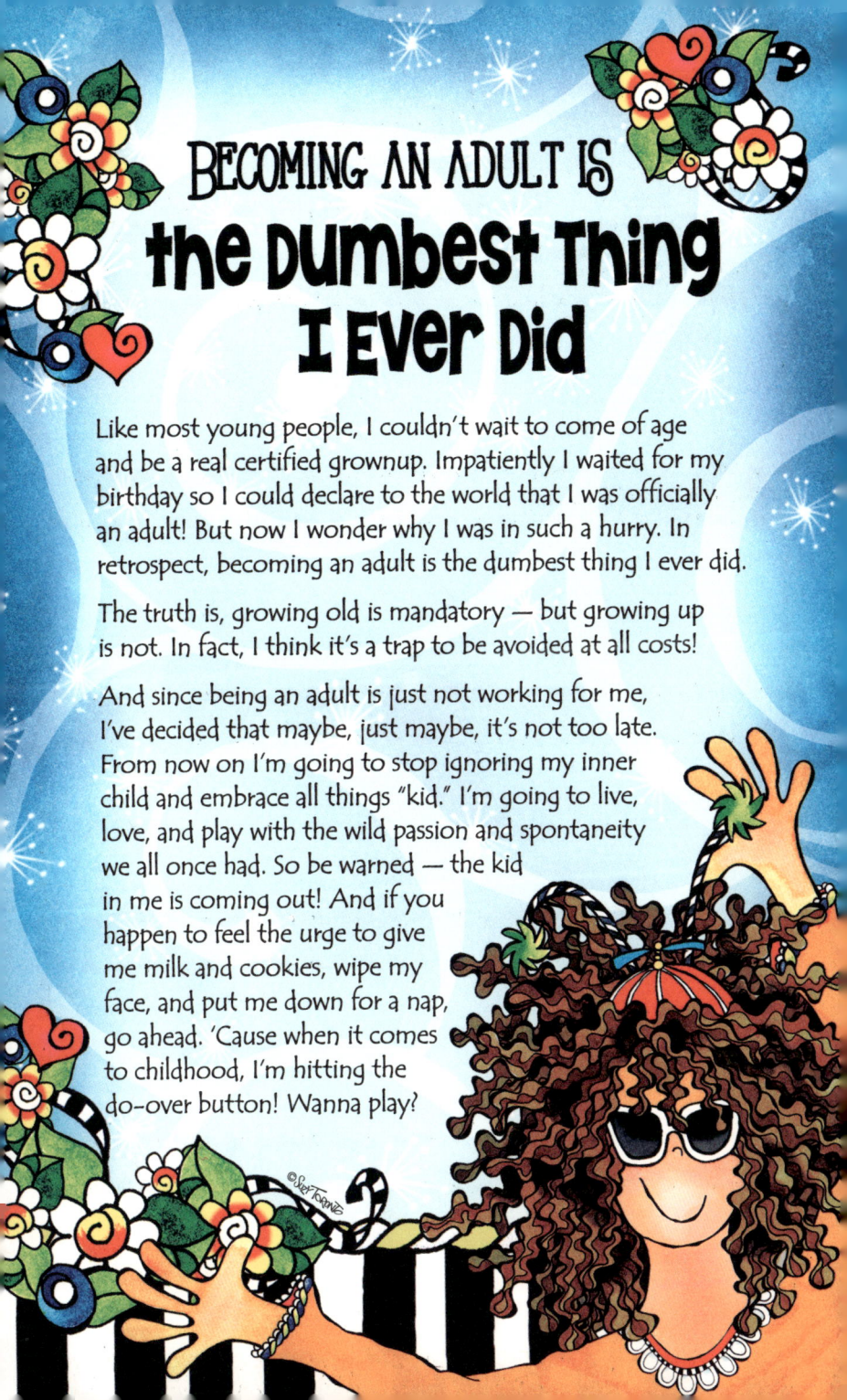

Naptime
is my happy hour.
(I'm done adulting!)

Sunday, June 28

Monday, June 29

Tuesday, June 30

Wednesday, July 1

Canada Day (Canada)

Thursday, July 2

Friday, July 3

Saturday, July 4

Independence Day (USA)

Notes:

I was
born to be **wild...**
but only until
9 p.m. or so!

July 2020

Sunday	Monday	Tuesday	Wednesday

June

S	M	T	W	T	F	S
	1	2	3	4	5	6
7	8	9	10	11	12	13
14	15	16	17	18	19	20
21	22	23	24	25	26	27
28	29	30				

August

S	M	T	W	T	F	S
						1
2	3	4	5	6	7	8
9	10	11	12	13	14	15
16	17	18	19	20	21	22
23/30	24/31	25	26	27	28	29

1
Canada Day (Canada)

5
Full Moon ○

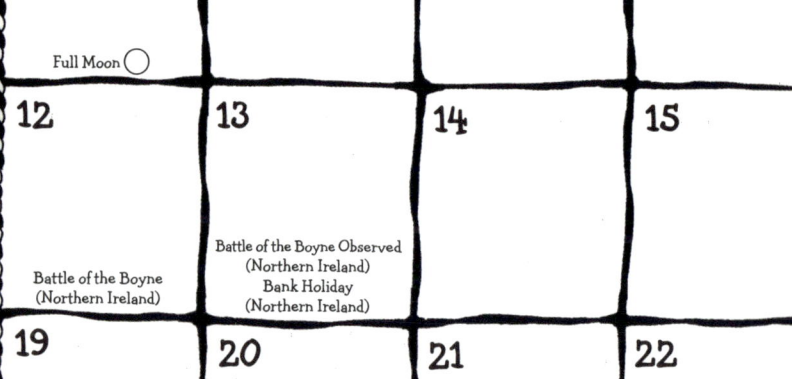

6

7

8

12
Battle of the Boyne
(Northern Ireland)

13
Battle of the Boyne Observed
(Northern Ireland)
Bank Holiday
(Northern Ireland)

14

15

19
National Ice Cream Day

20

21

22

26

27

28

29

Thursday	Friday	Saturday	Notes:
2	3	4 Independence Day (USA)	
9	10	11	
16	17	18	
23	24	25	
30	31 Eid al-Adha		

Sunday, July 5

Full Moon ○

Monday, July 6

Tuesday, July 7

Wednesday, July 8

Thursday, July 9

Friday, July 10

Saturday, July 11

Flip-Flops
Make Your Toes Feel like They're on
Vacation

We spend 95% of our time going through the motions of life, longing and yearning for the 5% that's left over. We call that 5% "vacation."

What if we could capture the concept of vacation with something so simple as a pair of flip-flops? We could slip them on, click our heels three times, and, in the blink of an eye, transport ourselves to a tropical isle. Women everywhere would rally in protest and throw out their sensible pumps. Flip-flops would become the new dress standard. The best part is that no matter where you are, you could wiggle your piggies, show off your pedicure, and turn that 5% into 100%! Flip-flops just make your toes feel like they're on vacation.

©Suzy Toronto

It's time to get into a
flip-flop state of mind.

Sunday, July 12

Battle of the Boyne (Northern Ireland)

Monday, July 13

Battle of the Boyne Observed (Northern Ireland)
Bank Holiday (Northern Ireland)

Tuesday, July 14

Wednesday, July 15

Thursday, July 16

Friday, July 17

Saturday, July 18

Notes:

It's hard to be
pompous and pretentious
when you're wearing
rubber flip-flops.

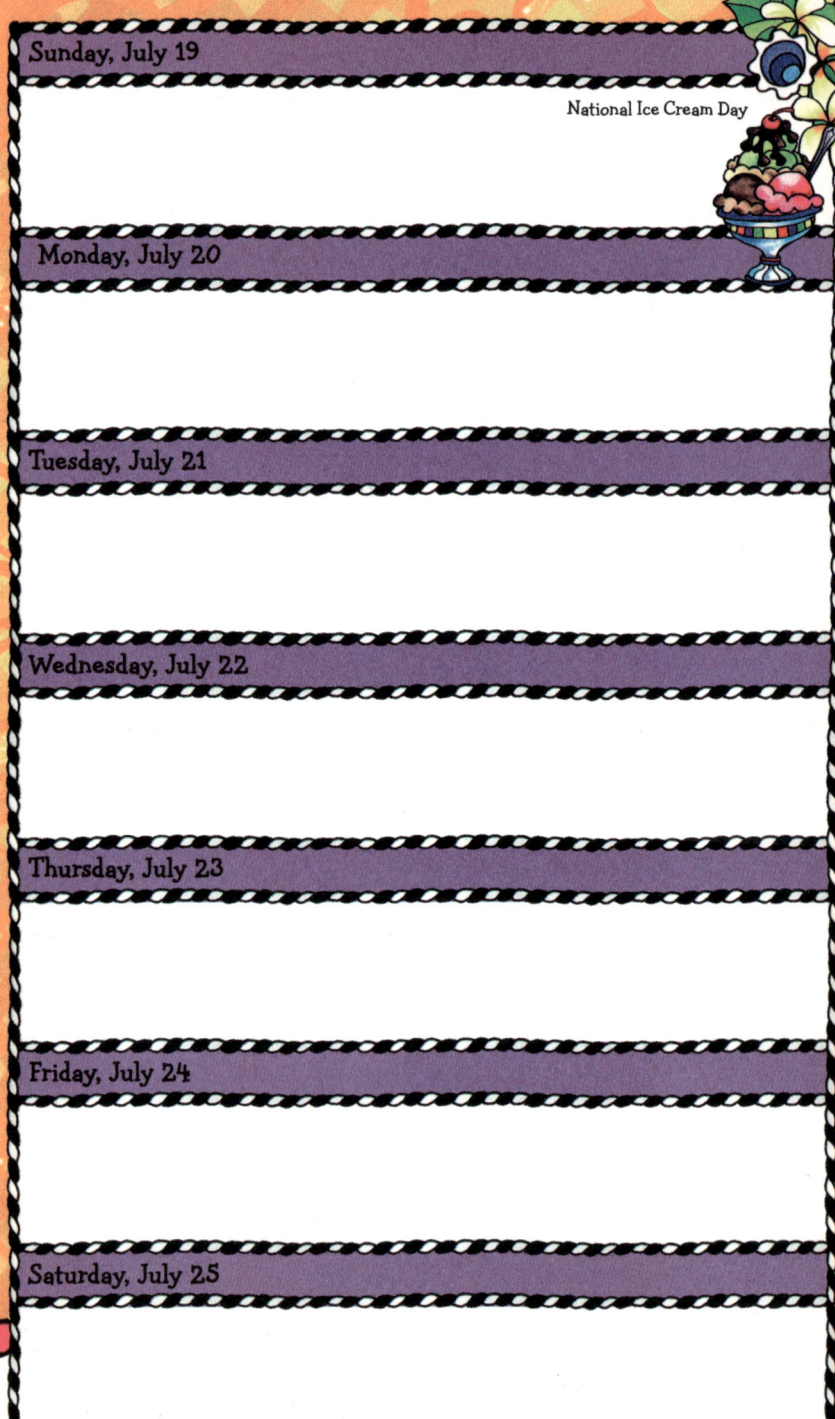

Sunday, July 19

National Ice Cream Day

Monday, July 20

Tuesday, July 21

Wednesday, July 22

Thursday, July 23

Friday, July 24

Saturday, July 25

Stop
What You're Doing and
Start Living

Have you ever noticed how few people really live their lives? They just seem to go through the motions, always waiting for next week or next month to give them a sense of relief. It's a trap that's far too easy to fall into. (I know. I've been there... more than once!)

So right this very second, take a deep breath... stop what you're doing... and start living. Let go of the chaos and choose to fully embrace every minute of your life. Proclaim today as your day and this very instant as your moment for the taking. This day will never come again. Next week will still come, deadlines will fly by, and appointments will come and go, but by tomorrow... today will be gone forever. So take a deep breath, let go, and LIVE!

©Suzy Toronto

Be responsible for the mojo you bring to the world.

Sunday, July 26

Monday, July 27

Tuesday, July 28

Wednesday, July 29

Thursday, July 30

Friday, July 31

Eid al-Adha

Saturday, August 1

Notes:

Embrace life for the wild, wacky, wonderful **adventure** it was always meant to be.

August 2020

Sunday	Monday	Tuesday	Wednesday

July

S	M	T	W	T	F	S
			1	2	3	4
5	6	7	8	9	10	11
12	13	14	15	16	17	18
19	20	21	22	23	24	25
26	27	28	29	30	31	

September

S	M	T	W	T	F	S
		1	2	3	4	5
6	7	8	9	10	11	12
13	14	15	16	17	18	19
20	21	22	23	24	25	26
27	28	29	30			

2

3
Civic Holiday (Canada)
Bank Holiday
(Ireland/Scotland)
Full Moon ○

4

5

9
National Women's Day
(South Africa)

10

11

12

16

17

18

19

23

24

25

26

30

31
Bank Holiday (UK
except Scotland)

Women's Equality Day (USA)

Thursday	Friday	Saturday	Notes:
		1	
6	7	8	
Wiggle Your Toes Day			
13	14	15	
20	21	22	
Islamic New Year			
27	28	29	

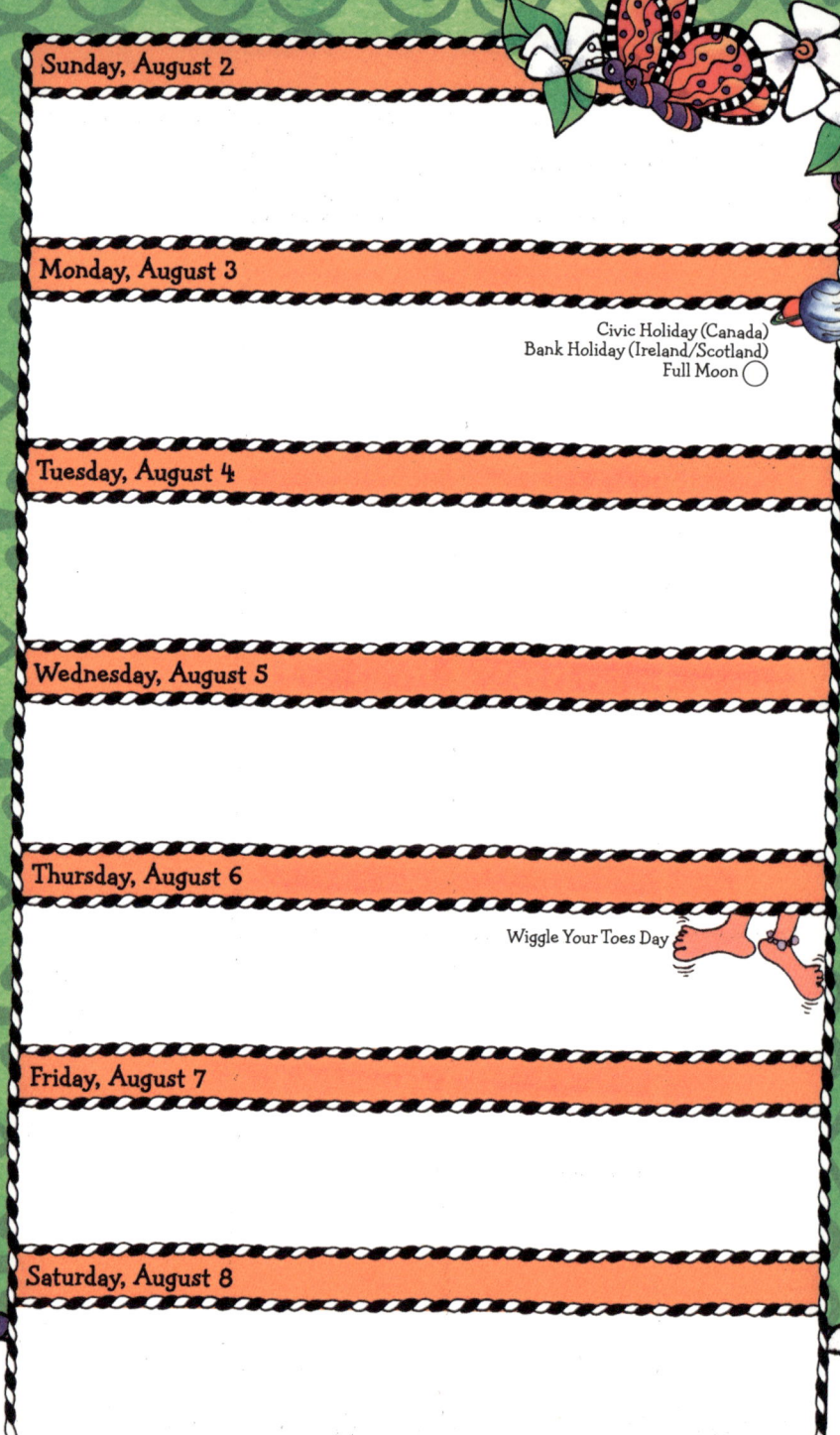

Sunday, August 2

Monday, August 3

Civic Holiday (Canada)
Bank Holiday (Ireland/Scotland)
Full Moon ◯

Tuesday, August 4

Wednesday, August 5

Thursday, August 6

Wiggle Your Toes Day

Friday, August 7

Saturday, August 8

...But I Like Being a
Drama Queen!

More than once, someone has rolled their eyes at me and told me to quit being such a drama queen. Instead of this stopping me in my tracks, that one short sentence makes me want to seize a can of spray adhesive with one hand and a jar of glitter with the other and say, "You're missing the whole point!" and then cover them with a lavish coat of sticky, iridescent bling.

But instead, I take a deep breath and I pray for the strength that I will never, ever listen to anyone who tells me to stop being myself. I then vow to forever breathe in the spark of passion that lights a fire in my soul and to always embrace the wild energy that makes my heart tingle.

You know it, I know it: sometimes we wonderful, wacky women need to empower our inner drama queens to help us create the excitement, passion, and fun that truly make our lives worth loving... no matter how many eyes are rolled along the way.

So stage your royal scene. Script out your passionate performance. And wear that crown with pride!

© Suzy Toronto

Drama

Empower the sparkle within you.

Sunday, August 9

National Women's Day (South Africa)

Monday, August 10

Tuesday, August 11

Wednesday, August 12

Thursday, August 13

Friday, August 14

Saturday, August 15

Notes:

Leave a trail of *Glitter* everywhere you go.

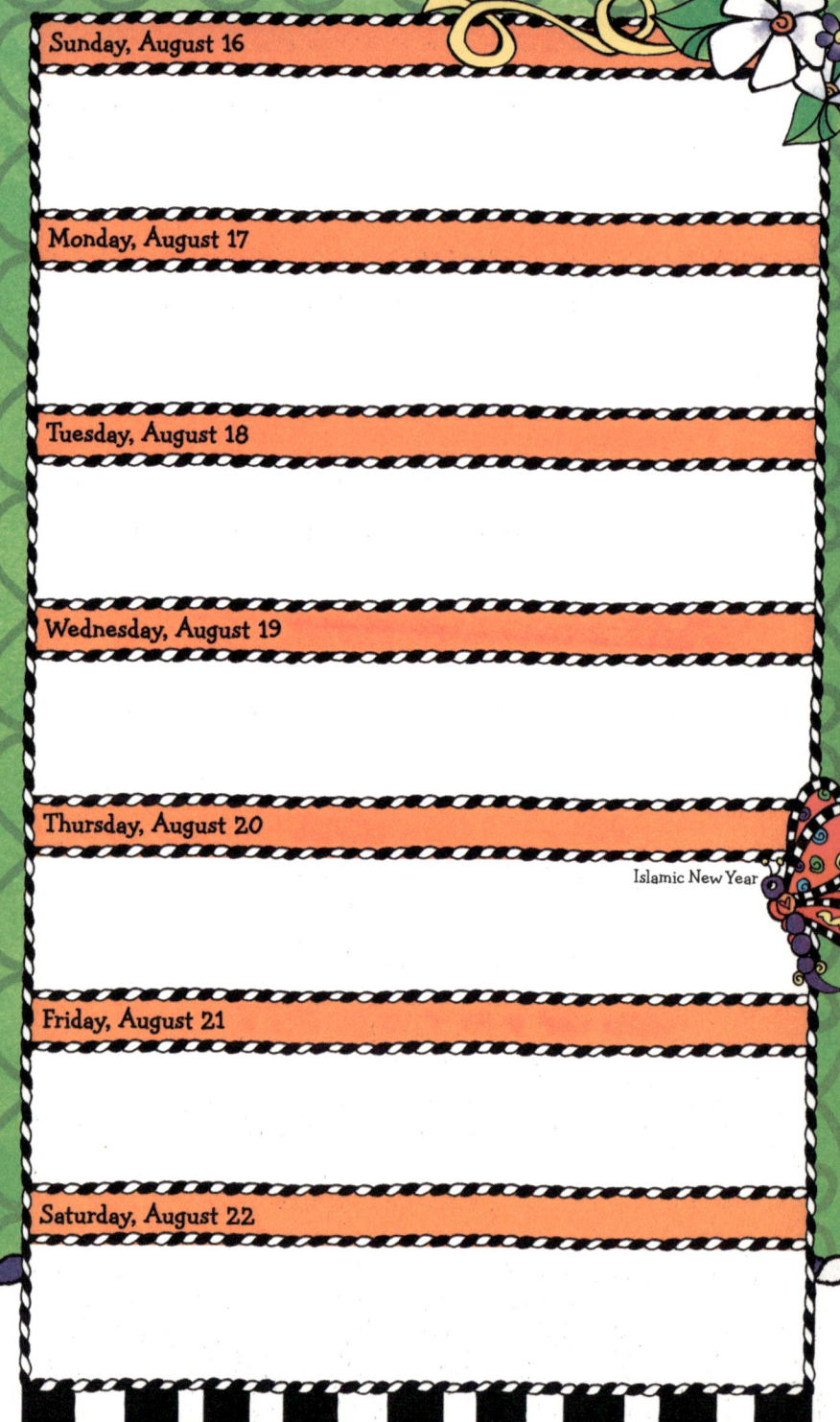

Sunday, August 16

Monday, August 17

Tuesday, August 18

Wednesday, August 19

Thursday, August 20

Islamic New Year

Friday, August 21

Saturday, August 22

Don't Let Your Frame of Mind Frame you In

Have you ever felt like doing something totally wacky, like dancing in a fountain… fully clothed… in the middle of the day… with people everywhere? I've seen someone do it, and the laughter and smiles tell you in a minute that the scene has just made everyone's day. Most of us have crazy thoughts like that, but we don't act on them. Our frame of mind frames us in. It dampens our growth and creativity, and wreaks havoc with our imagination. Daring to be wacky means reaching out of our comfort zone and taking a chance. Sure, it's risky — but so what? Being a wacky woman means following your heart. You don't have to be obnoxious or extreme; just be willing to let go of your doubts and grab hold of the first opportunity that comes your way.

Take music lessons. Go back to school. Make friends with an old rival. Volunteer for charity. Run a race. Try out for a play. Join a hula class. The results will amaze you. You're never too old, too young, too rich, or too poor to just do it.

Ready? Set. Go!

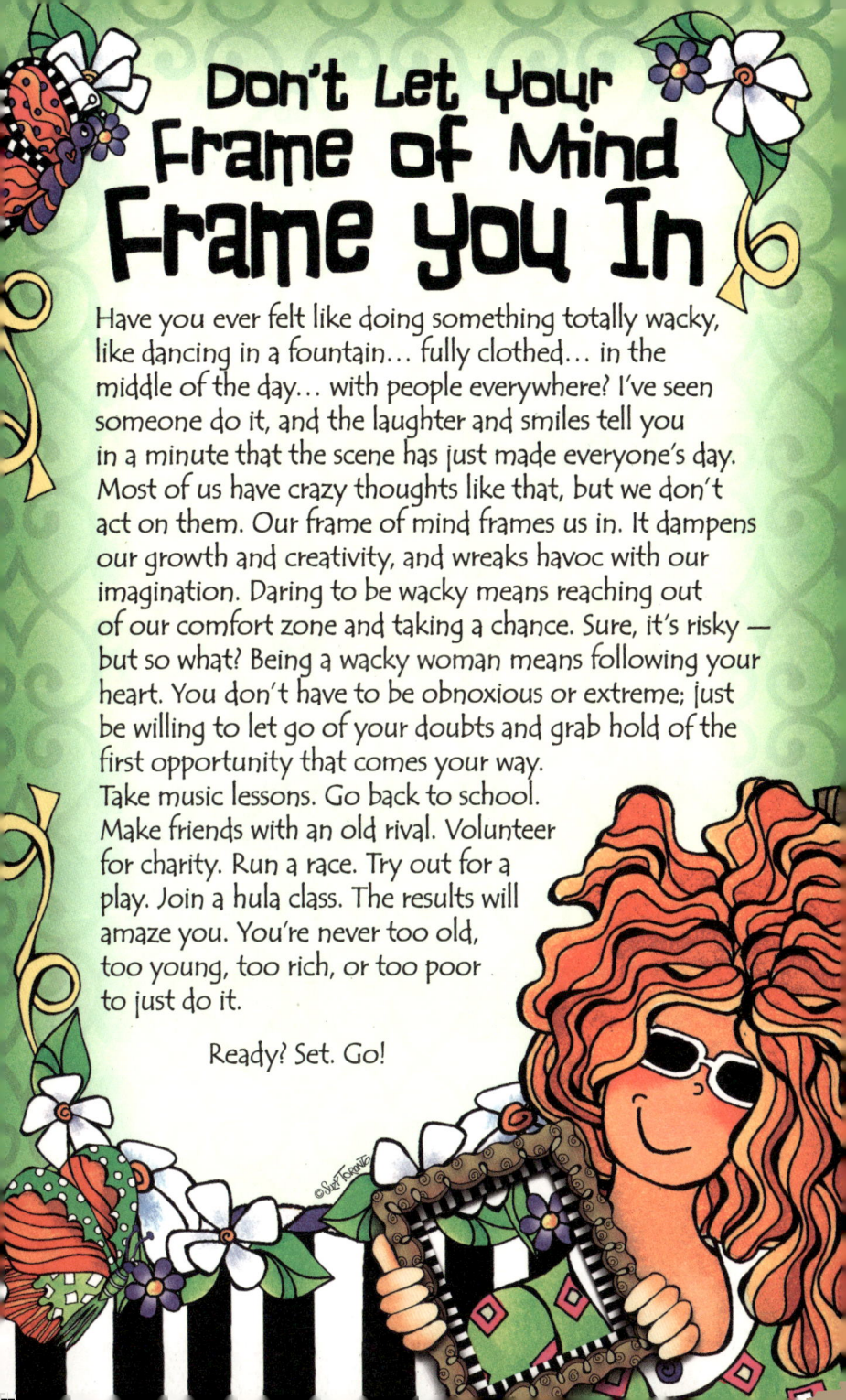

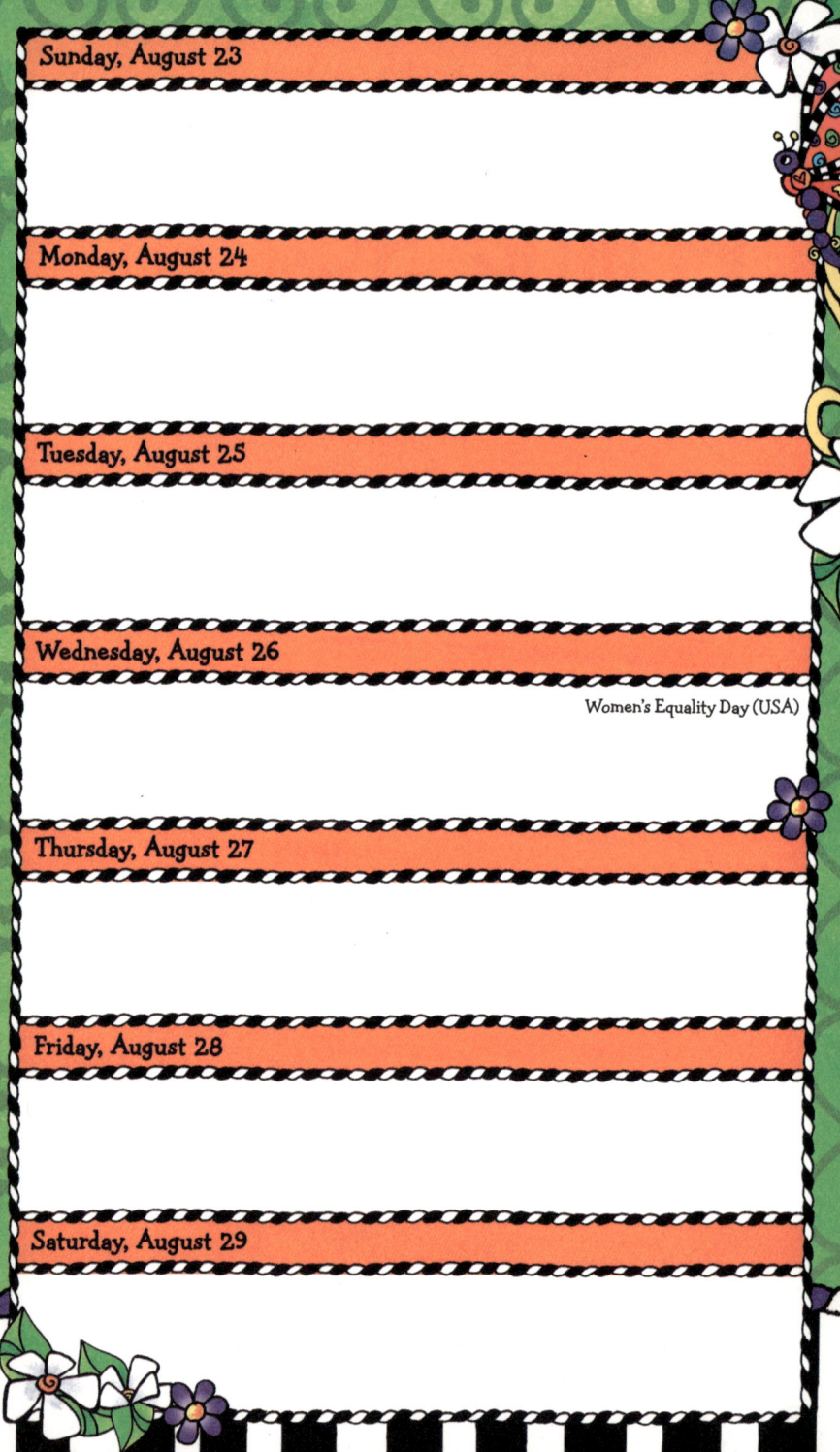

Sunday, August 23

Monday, August 24

Tuesday, August 25

Wednesday, August 26

Women's Equality Day (USA)

Thursday, August 27

Friday, August 28

Saturday, August 29

Sunday, August 30

Monday, August 31

Bank Holiday (UK except Scotland)

Tuesday, September 1

Wednesday, September 2

Secretaries' Day (South Africa)
Full Moon

Thursday, September 3

Friday, September 4

Saturday, September 5

September 2020

Sunday	Monday	Tuesday	Wednesday
		1	2 Secretaries' Day (South Africa) Full Moon ○
6	7 Labor Day (USA/Canada)	8	9
13 National Grandparents Day (USA)	14	15	16
20	21 UN International Day of Peace	22 Autumn Begins	23
27	28 Yom Kippur	29	30

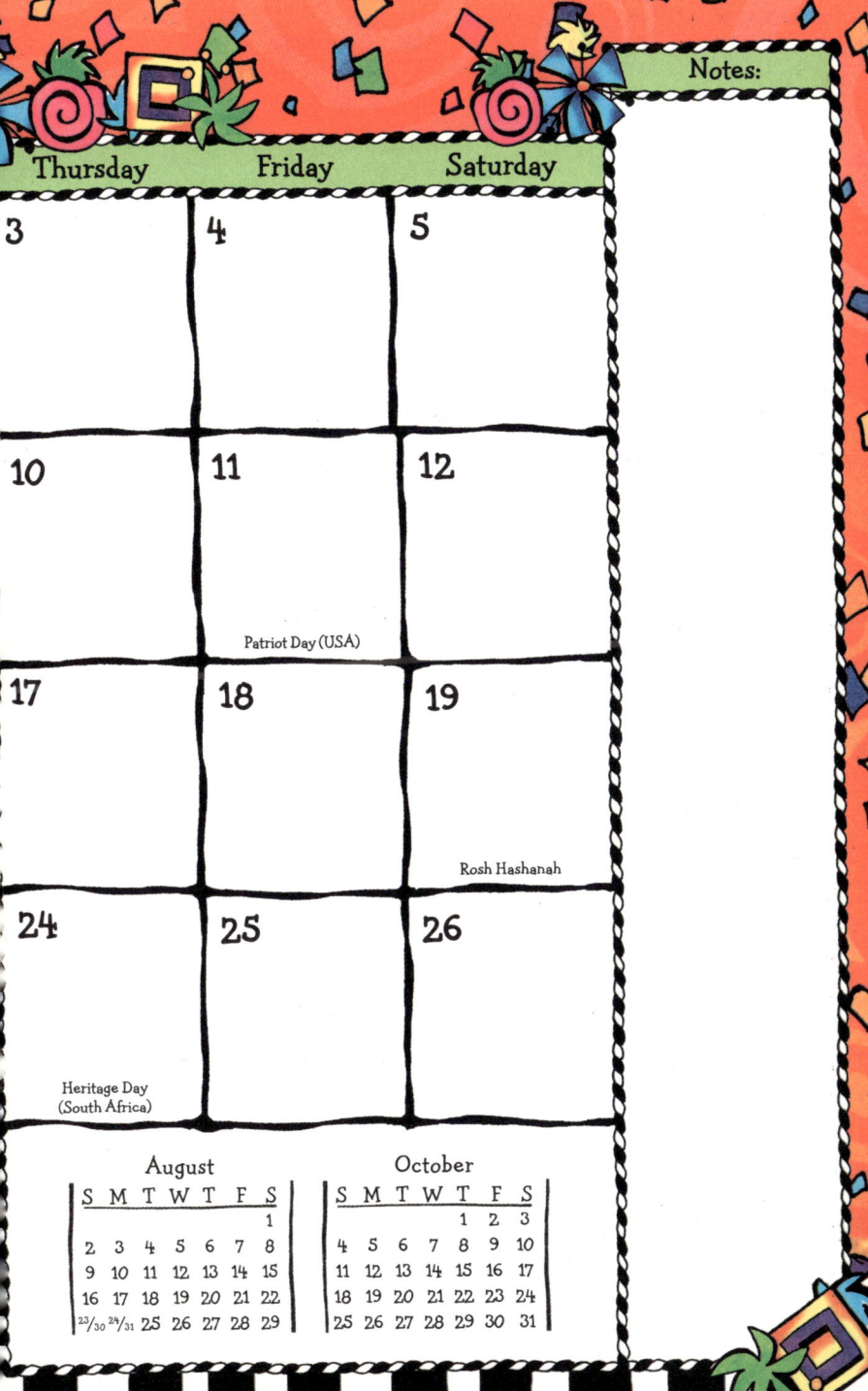

Thursday	Friday	Saturday
3	4	5
10	11 Patriot Day (USA)	12
17	18	19 Rosh Hashanah
24 Heritage Day (South Africa)	25	26

Notes:

August
S	M	T	W	T	F	S
						1
2	3	4	5	6	7	8
9	10	11	12	13	14	15
16	17	18	19	20	21	22
23/30	24/31	25	26	27	28	29

October
S	M	T	W	T	F	S
				1	2	3
4	5	6	7	8	9	10
11	12	13	14	15	16	17
18	19	20	21	22	23	24
25	26	27	28	29	30	31

Sunday, September 6

Monday, September 7

Labor Day (USA/Canada)

Tuesday, September 8

Wednesday, September 9

Thursday, September 10

Friday, September 11

Patriot Day (USA)

Saturday, September 12

When You Stumble, Make It Part of the Dance

Everyone messes up. It's part of the dance of life. There's simply no way to avoid all the obstacles, and it's inevitable that we'll stumble. Despite the fact that the music plays on, we find ourselves out of step and desperately searching for a do-over button.

That's when creativity and adaptability become our most valuable, lifesaving virtues. They help us muster up the courage to carry on and simply act as if it were all part of the show... even though behind the scenes our pride may have been battered and bruised. Without offering apologies, excuses, or explanations, we discover that it's just a matter of continuing onward with all our heart and soul as if our lives depended on it.

So the next time you stumble, smile at the crowd, kick up your heels, and dance a jig! The moment you embrace it as your own, no one will know it's not part of *your* dance.

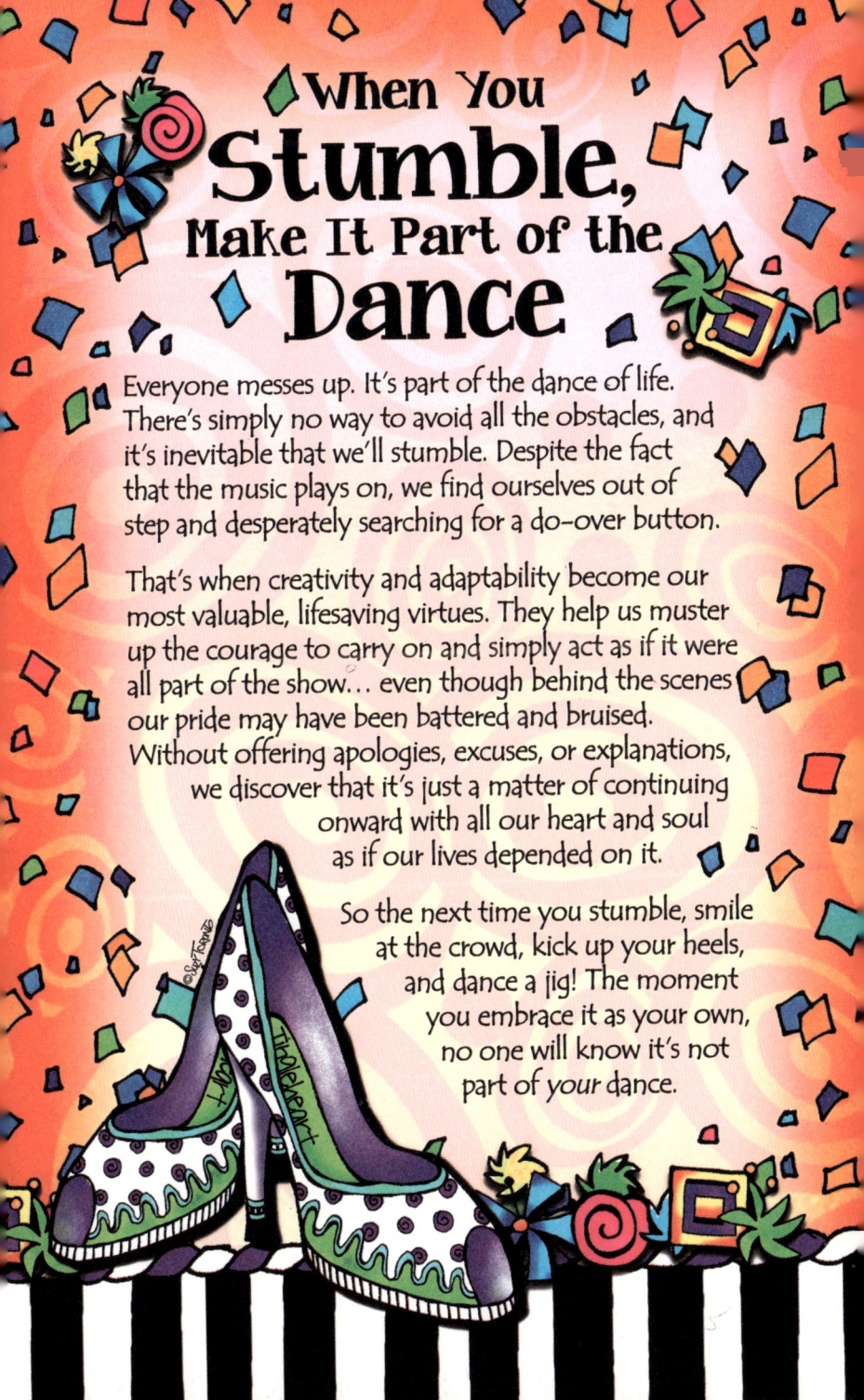

March to your own beat.

Sunday, September 13

National Grandparents Day (USA)

Monday, September 14

Tuesday, September 15

Wednesday, September 16

Thursday, September 17

Friday, September 18

Saturday, September 19

Rosh Hashanah

Notes:

Never let a stumble
in the road be
the end of your journey.
Keep skipping along!

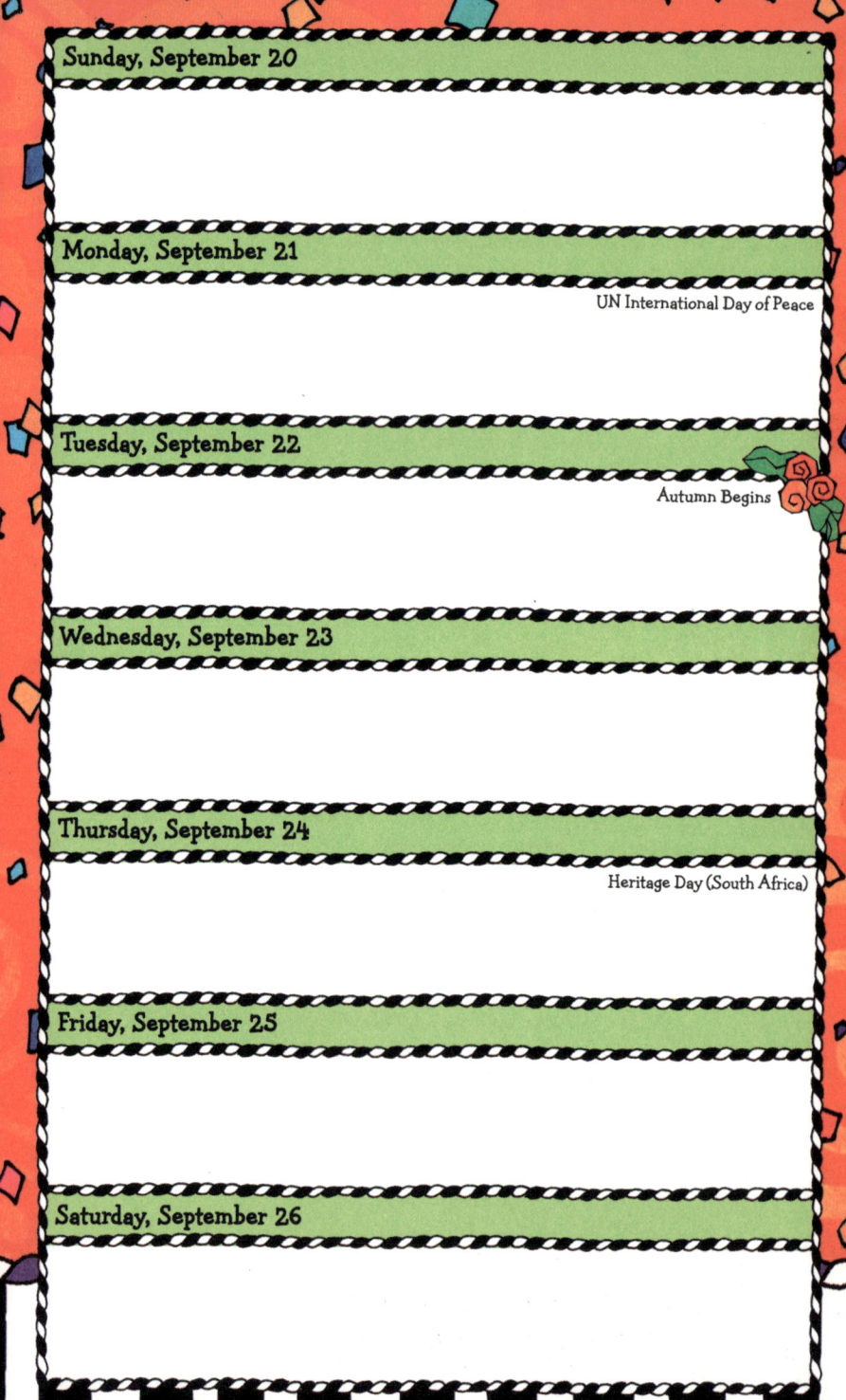

Sunday, September 20

Monday, September 21

UN International Day of Peace

Tuesday, September 22

Autumn Begins

Wednesday, September 23

Thursday, September 24

Heritage Day (South Africa)

Friday, September 25

Saturday, September 26

Sometimes My Life Is Only One Tent Away from
a Full-Blown Circus

Some days there is just no denying it. Your life starts to resemble a full-blown, over-the-top, three-ring circus… and a poorly run one at that! With your arms flailing, hair flying, and screaming at the top of your lungs, passersby might even think you're a daring trapeze artist attempting her first trick!

But guess what? You are not alone. Up and down your street, around each corner, and behind closed doors, at some point most of us have also had the same experience.

So if life is going to be a circus, rally your friends, step right up, and make it the greatest show on earth… the likes of which the world has never known. Once you do, you'll find that your troubles are easier when you embrace them with friends. And if there happens to be an elephant in the corner of the room, introduce her and let her perform!

It's time to hoist up that big tent, march in the menagerie, and let the show begin. It's going to be stupendous!

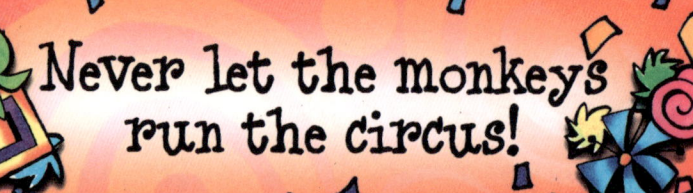

Never let the monkeys
run the circus!

Sunday, September 27

Monday, September 28

Yom Kippur

Tuesday, September 29

Wednesday, September 30

Thursday, October 1

National Breast Cancer Awareness Month Begins (USA)
Full Moon ○

Friday, October 2

Saturday, October 3

First Day of Succoth

Notes:

Some days you're cleaning up after the monkeys...

but other days you get to fly on the trapeze!

October 2020

Sunday	Monday	Tuesday	Wednesday

4	5	6	7
Grandparents Day (South Africa)			
11	12	13	14
	Columbus Day Observed (USA) Thanksgiving Day (Canada)		
18	19	20	21
25	26	27	28
UK/Ireland Daylight Saving Time Ends	Bank Holiday (Ireland)		

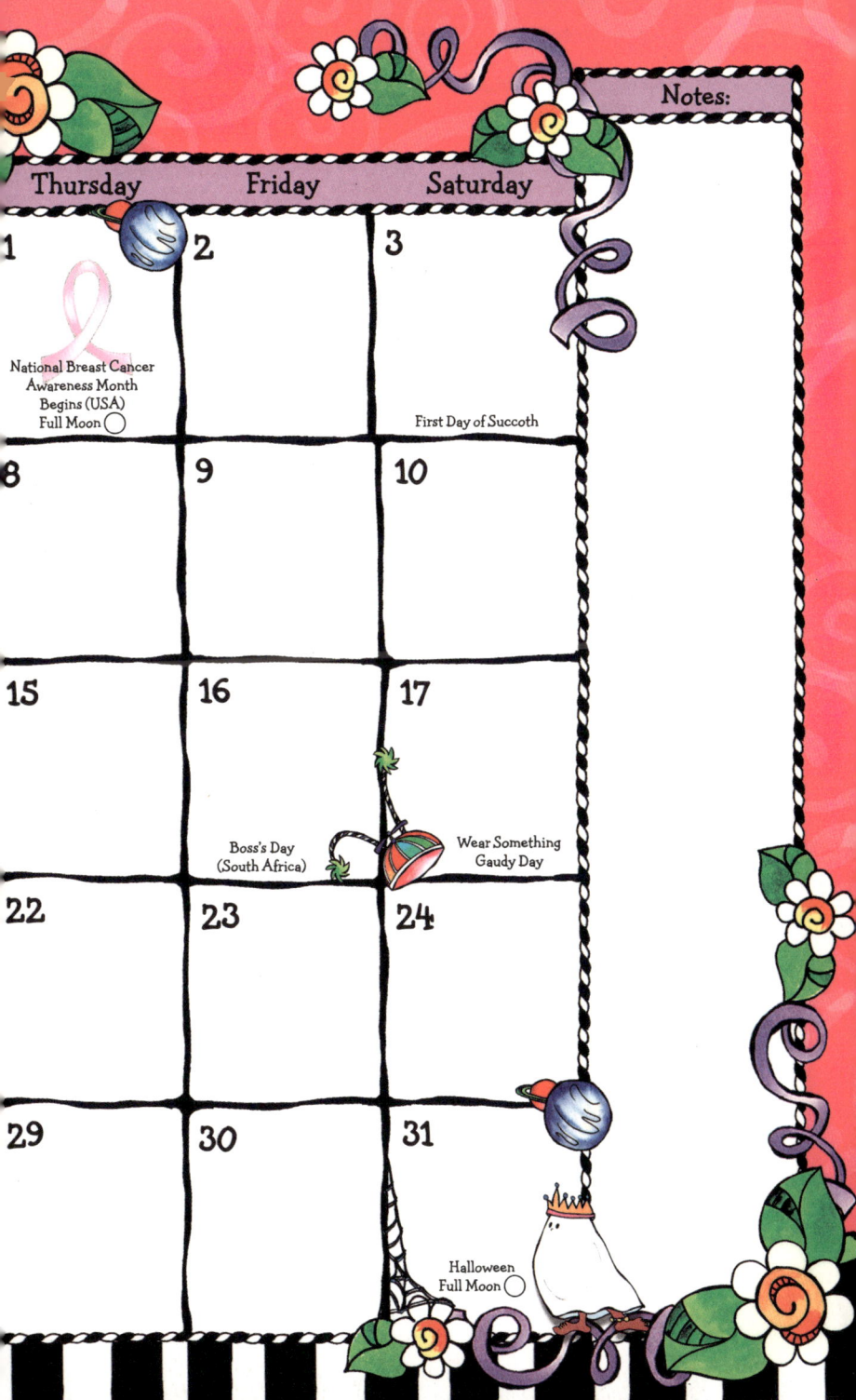

Thursday	Friday	Saturday
1 National Breast Cancer Awareness Month Begins (USA) Full Moon ○	**2**	**3** First Day of Succoth
8	**9**	**10**
15	**16** Boss's Day (South Africa)	**17** Wear Something Gaudy Day
22	**23**	**24**
29	**30**	**31** Halloween Full Moon ○

Notes:

Sunday, October 4

Grandparents Day (South Africa)

Monday, October 5

Tuesday, October 6

Wednesday, October 7

Thursday, October 8

Friday, October 9

Saturday, October 10

As a Matter of Fact, I Do Need Another Pair of Shoes

I never tell him he has too many tools, cars, or golf clubs. So why does he think I have too many pairs of shoes? Actually, it's not my fault. It's a genetic predisposition carved deep into my DNA. And to make matters worse, those insensitive shoe manufacturers prey on my disability, making such temptingly adorable shoes that I simply can't resist. I'm telling you… it's totally out of my control. Okay, so I have a few pairs of shoes… all right, maybe more than a few. But cute shoes are my therapy, and I must have them to survive! Besides, they are not immoral, illegal, or fattening, and they make my heart tingle.
So, yes, as a matter of fact, I *do* need another pair of shoes!

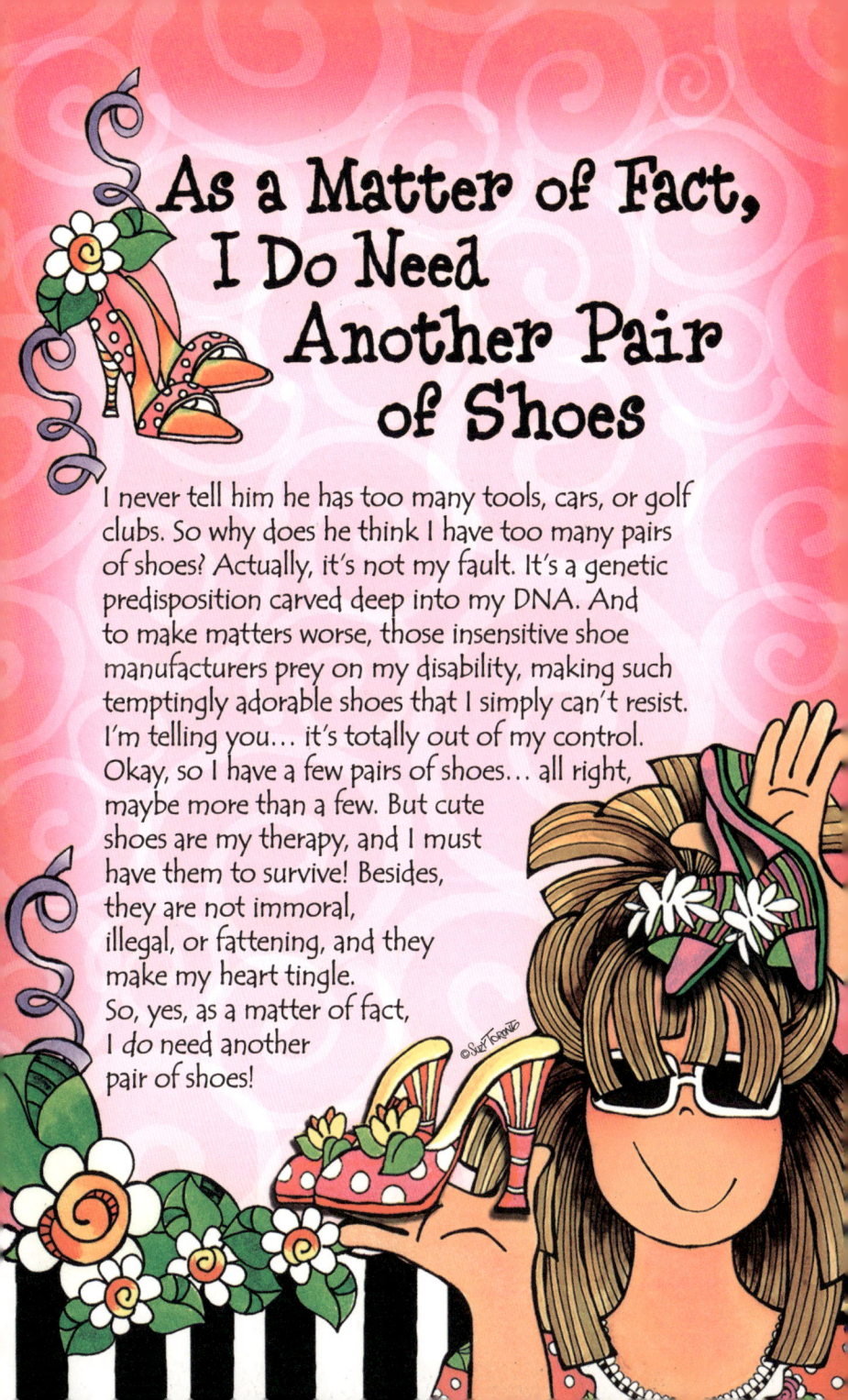

Cute shoes make my heart tingle.

Sunday October 11

Monday, October 12

Columbus Day Observed (USA)
Thanksgiving Day (Canada)

Tuesday, October 13

Wednesday, October 14

Thursday, October 15

Friday, October 16

Boss's Day (South Africa)

Saturday, October 17

Wear Something Gaudy Day

Notes:

Cute Shoes:
Cheaper than therapy and a whole lot more fun!

Sunday, October 18

Monday, October 19

Tuesday, October 20

Wednesday, October 21

Thursday, October 22

Friday, October 23

Saturday, October 24

I'm Feeling Diagonally Parked in a Parallel Universe

Yeah, I know… I've heard it all before. "You're not like the rest of your family." Folks always seem to be amazed that a quick spin of the genetic roulette wheel flung me out of what was otherwise a pretty normal bunch of people.

And no, I'm not the black sheep of my family… although I have been accused of being the wacky tie-dyed one with polka dots! It's just that I look at the world with a different perspective than most. My world is filled with wild colors, creative energy, and large amounts of emotional glitter that sometimes explode at slightly inopportune times. This wonderful wacky viewpoint allows me to skip through life with my own syncopated gait. For me, it's 100% authentic and true, and it's not about being a rebel or trying to prove anything.

So yes, if you accuse me of being diagonally parked in a parallel universe, you'd be absolutely right! But it's an upside-down, inside-out reality that suits me just fine. And it's okay to pull in and diagonally park beside me. There's plenty of room for you too. Welcome to my world!

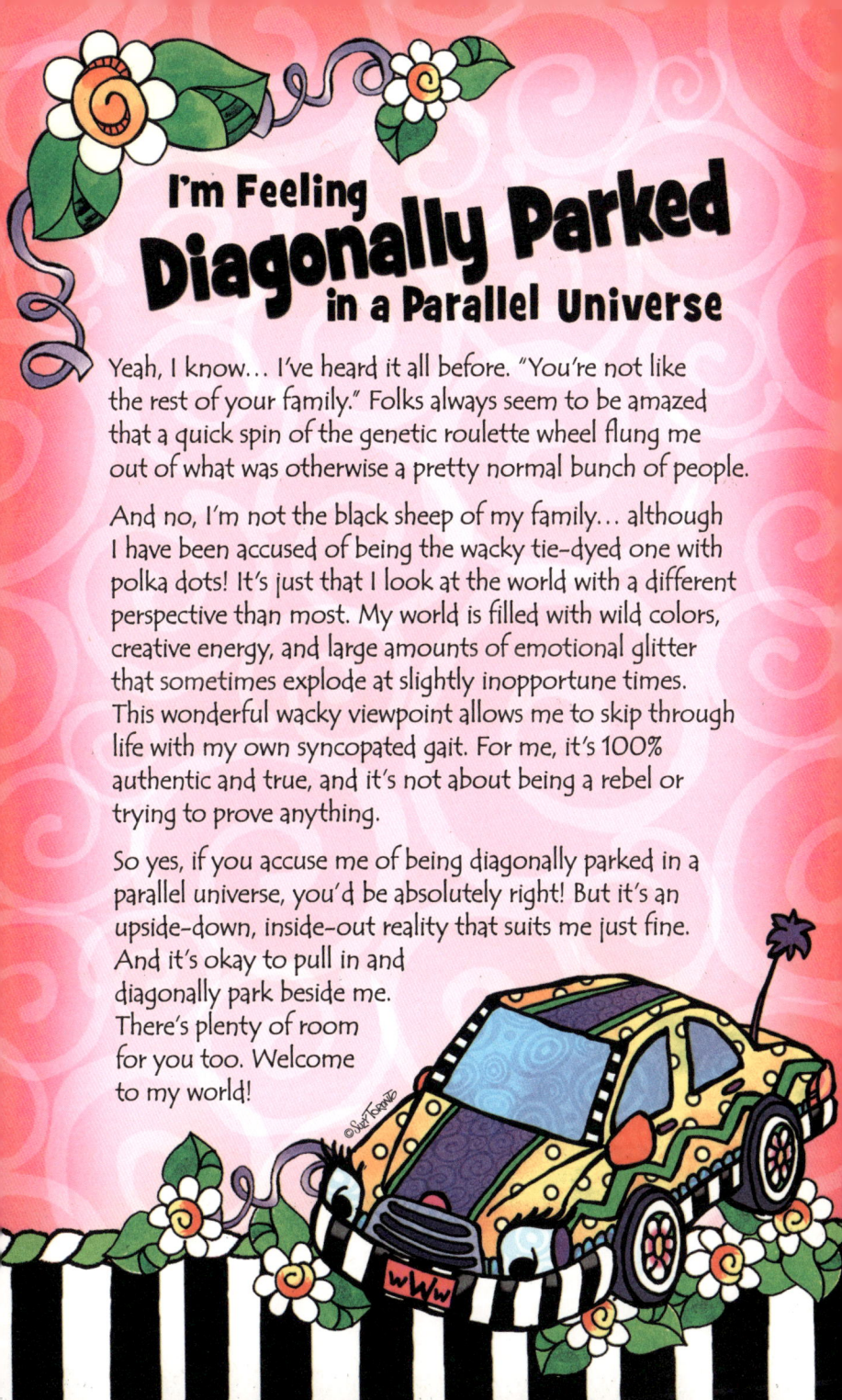

Let go of the status quo and just be yourself!

Sunday, October 25

UK/Ireland Daylight Saving Time Ends

Monday, October 26

Bank Holiday (Ireland)

Tuesday, October 27

Wednesday, October 28

Thursday, October 29

Friday, October 30

Saturday, October 31

Halloween
Full Moon ○

Notes:

Being a
Wonderful Wacky Woman
is no big thing.

It's a zillion little things
and you're doing them
all just right!

November 2020

Sunday	Monday	Tuesday	Wednesday
1 USA/Canada Daylight Saving Time Ends	2	3 **VOTE** Election Day (USA)	4
8 Remembrance Sunday (UK)	9	10	11 HERO Veterans Day (USA) Remembrance Day (Canada/Australia)
15	16	17	18
22	23	24	25
29	30 St. Andrew's Day (Scotland) Full Moon ○		

Thursday	Friday	Saturday
5	6	7
Guy Fawkes Day (UK)		
12	13	14
		Diwali (South Africa)
19	20	21
26	27	28
Thanksgiving Day (USA)		

Notes:

October

S	M	T	W	T	F	S
				1	2	3
4	5	6	7	8	9	10
11	12	13	14	15	16	17
18	19	20	21	22	23	24
25	26	27	28	29	30	31

December

S	M	T	W	T	F	S
		1	2	3	4	5
6	7	8	9	10	11	12
13	14	15	16	17	18	19
20	21	22	23	24	25	26
27	28	29	30	31		

Sunday, November 1

USA/Canada Daylight Saving Time Ends

Monday, November 2

Tuesday, November 3

Election Day (USA)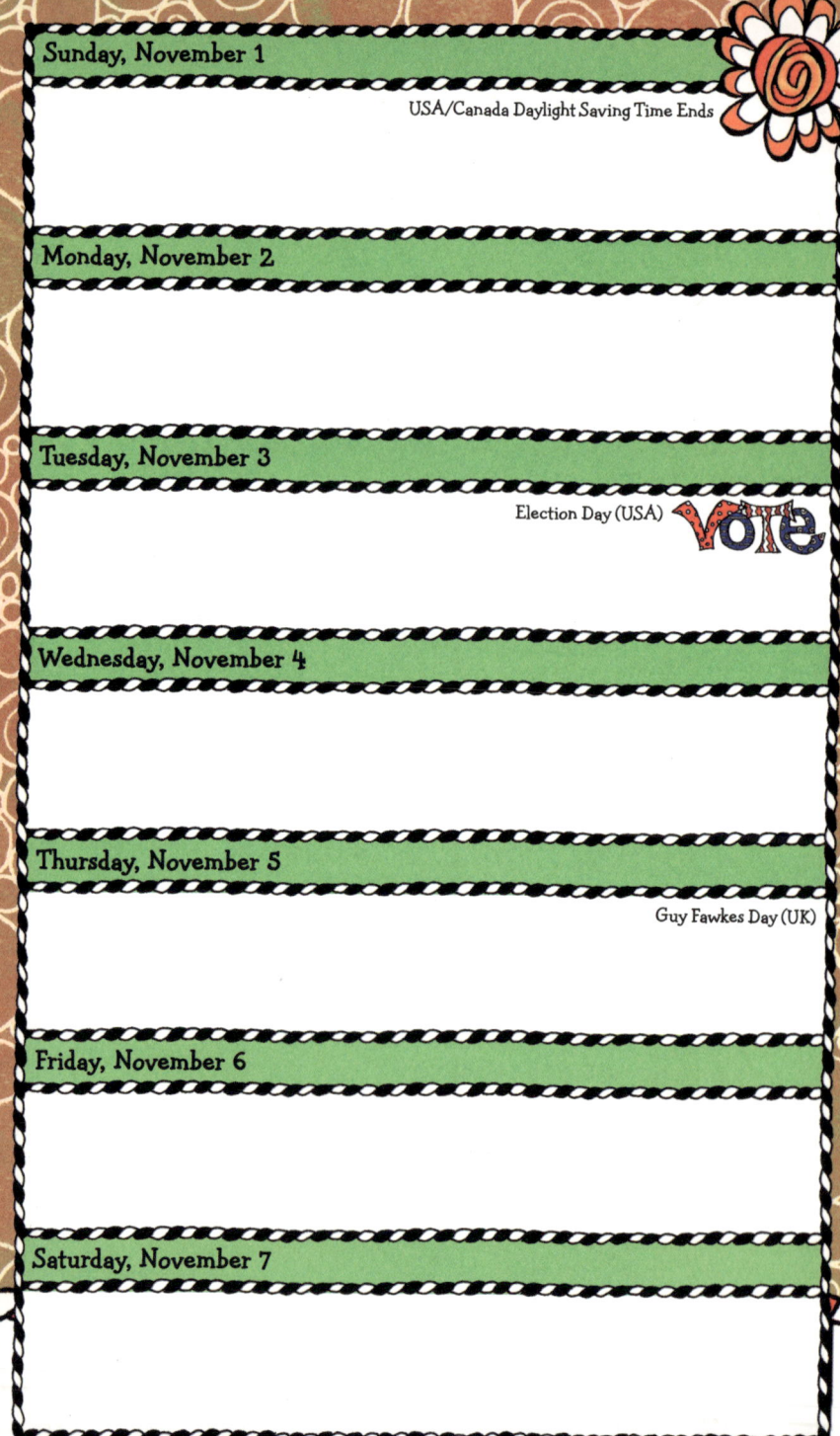

Wednesday, November 4

Thursday, November 5

Guy Fawkes Day (UK)

Friday, November 6

Saturday, November 7

Follow Your Dreams...
with Your Arms Flailing, Hair Flying, and Screaming at the Top of *Your Lungs!*

Do not take the advice of those old sages and wait until you can "walk confidently in the direction of your dreams." If you do, you'll never take the first step. Instead, leap and learn to fly on the way down. (And for heaven's sake, don't think you have to wait until you lose ten pounds!)

Now is the time to jump in with both feet... arms flailing, hair flying, and screaming at the top of your lungs, "I can do this!"

You don't have to believe it...
you just have to do it.
So don't wait
a minute longer.
Start now!

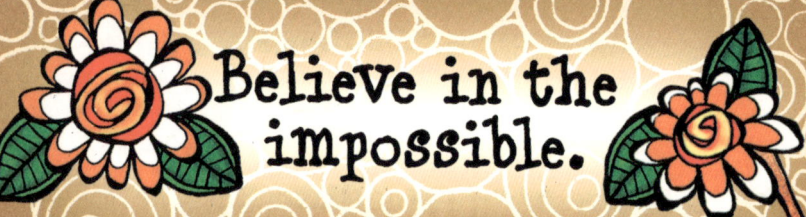

Believe in the impossible.

Sunday, November 8

Remembrance Sunday (UK)

Monday, November 9

Tuesday, November 10

Wednesday, November 11

Veterans Day (USA)
Remembrance Day (Canada/Australia)

Thursday, November 12

Friday, November 13

Saturday, November 14

Diwali (South Africa)

Notes:

Dream in colors
that do not
yet exist.

Sunday, November 15

Monday, November 16

Tuesday, November 17

Wednesday, November 18

Thursday, November 19

Friday, November 20

Saturday, November 21

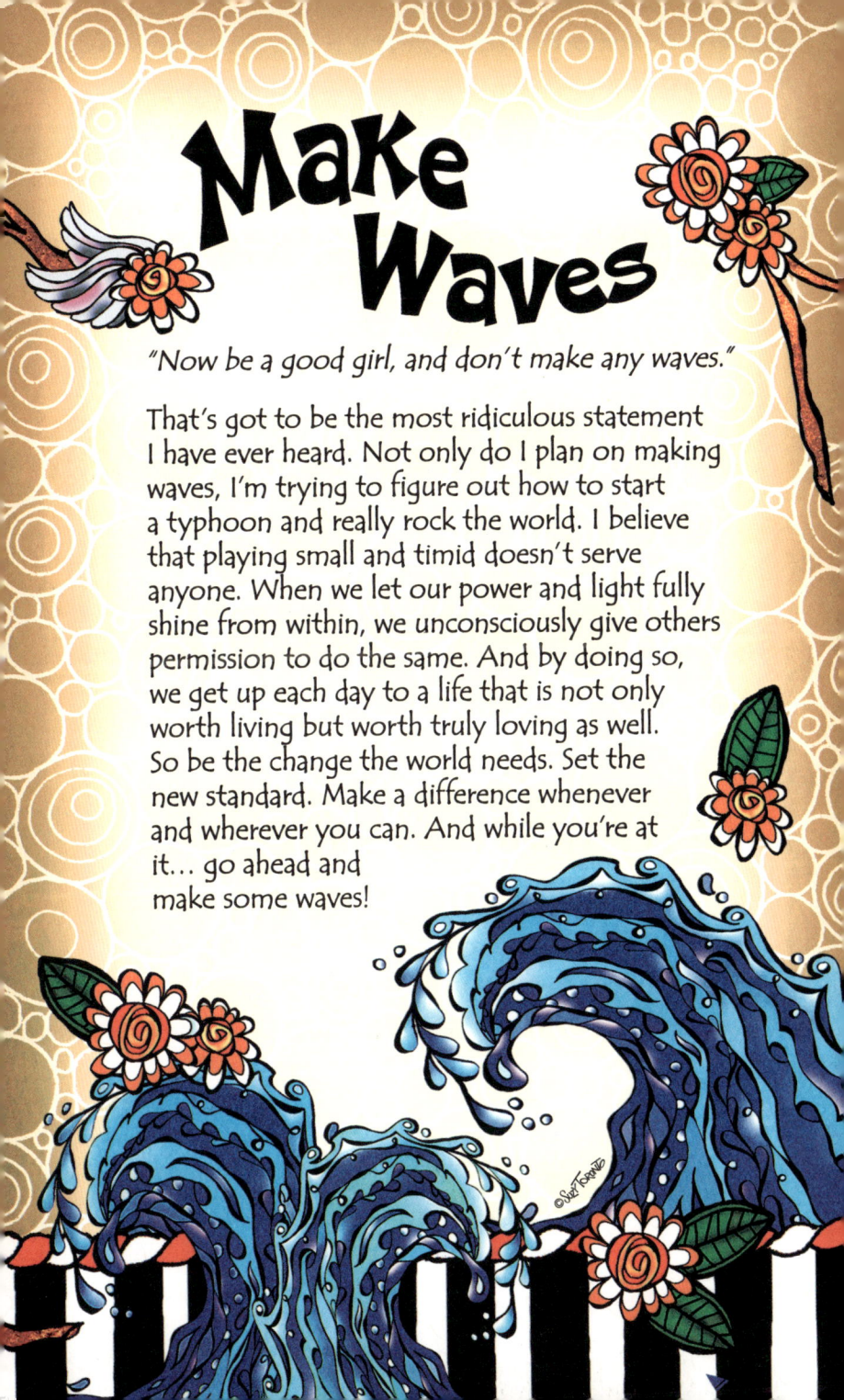

Make Waves

"Now be a good girl, and don't make any waves."

That's got to be the most ridiculous statement I have ever heard. Not only do I plan on making waves, I'm trying to figure out how to start a typhoon and really rock the world. I believe that playing small and timid doesn't serve anyone. When we let our power and light fully shine from within, we unconsciously give others permission to do the same. And by doing so, we get up each day to a life that is not only worth living but worth truly loving as well. So be the change the world needs. Set the new standard. Make a difference whenever and wherever you can. And while you're at it… go ahead and make some waves!

Sunday, November 22

Monday, November 23

Tuesday, November 24

Wednesday, November 25

Thursday, November 26

Thanksgiving Day (USA)

Friday, November 27

Saturday, November 28

Sunday, November 29

Monday, November 30

St. Andrew's Day (Scotland)
Full Moon ◯

Tuesday, December 1

Wednesday, December 2

Thursday, December 3

Friday, December 4

Saturday, December 5

December 2020

Sunday	Monday	Tuesday	Wednesday
		1	**2**
6	**7** National Pearl Harbor Remembrance Day (USA)	**8**	**9**
13	**14**	**15**	**16** National Chocolate-Covered Anything Day Day of Reconciliation (South Africa)
20	**21** Winter Begins	**22**	**23**
27	**28** Bank Holiday (UK) St. Stephen's Day Observed (Ireland)	**29** Full Moon ○	**30**

November

S	M	T	W	T	F	S
1	2	3	4	5	6	7
8	9	10	11	12	13	14
15	16	17	18	19	20	21
22	23	24	25	26	27	28
29	30					

January 2021

S	M	T	W	T	F	S
					1	2
3	4	5	6	7	8	9
10	11	12	13	14	15	16
17	18	19	20	21	22	23
24/31	25	26	27	28	29	30

Thursday	Friday	Saturday	Notes:
3	4	5	
10	11	12	
	First Day of Hanukkah		
17	18	19	
24	25	26	
Christmas Eve	Christmas	First Day of Kwanzaa (USA) Boxing Day (Canada/UK/Australia) St. Stephen's Day (Ireland) Day of Goodwill (South Africa)	
31			
New Year's Eve			

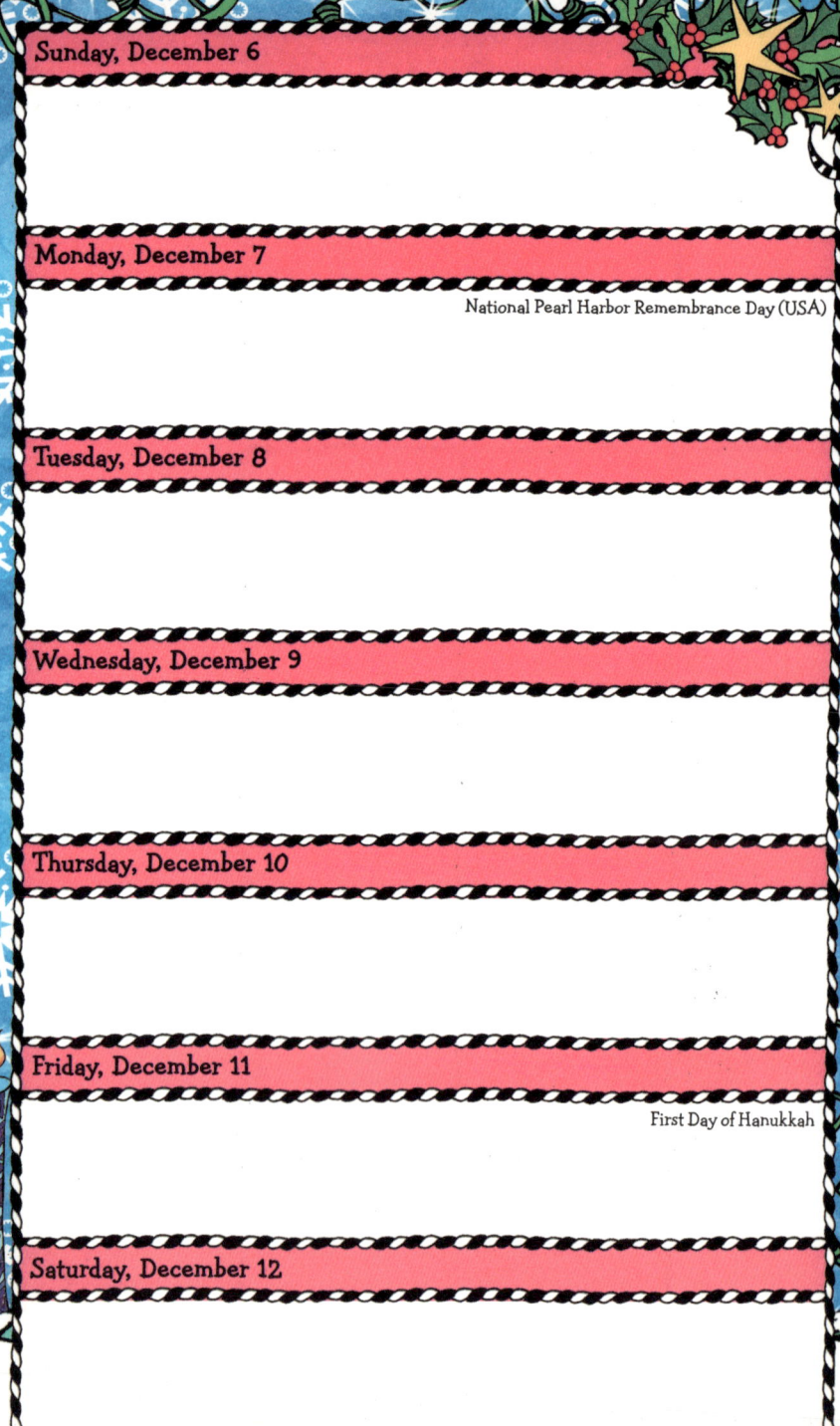

Sunday, December 6

Monday, December 7

National Pearl Harbor Remembrance Day (USA)

Tuesday, December 8

Wednesday, December 9

Thursday, December 10

Friday, December 11

First Day of Hanukkah

Saturday, December 12

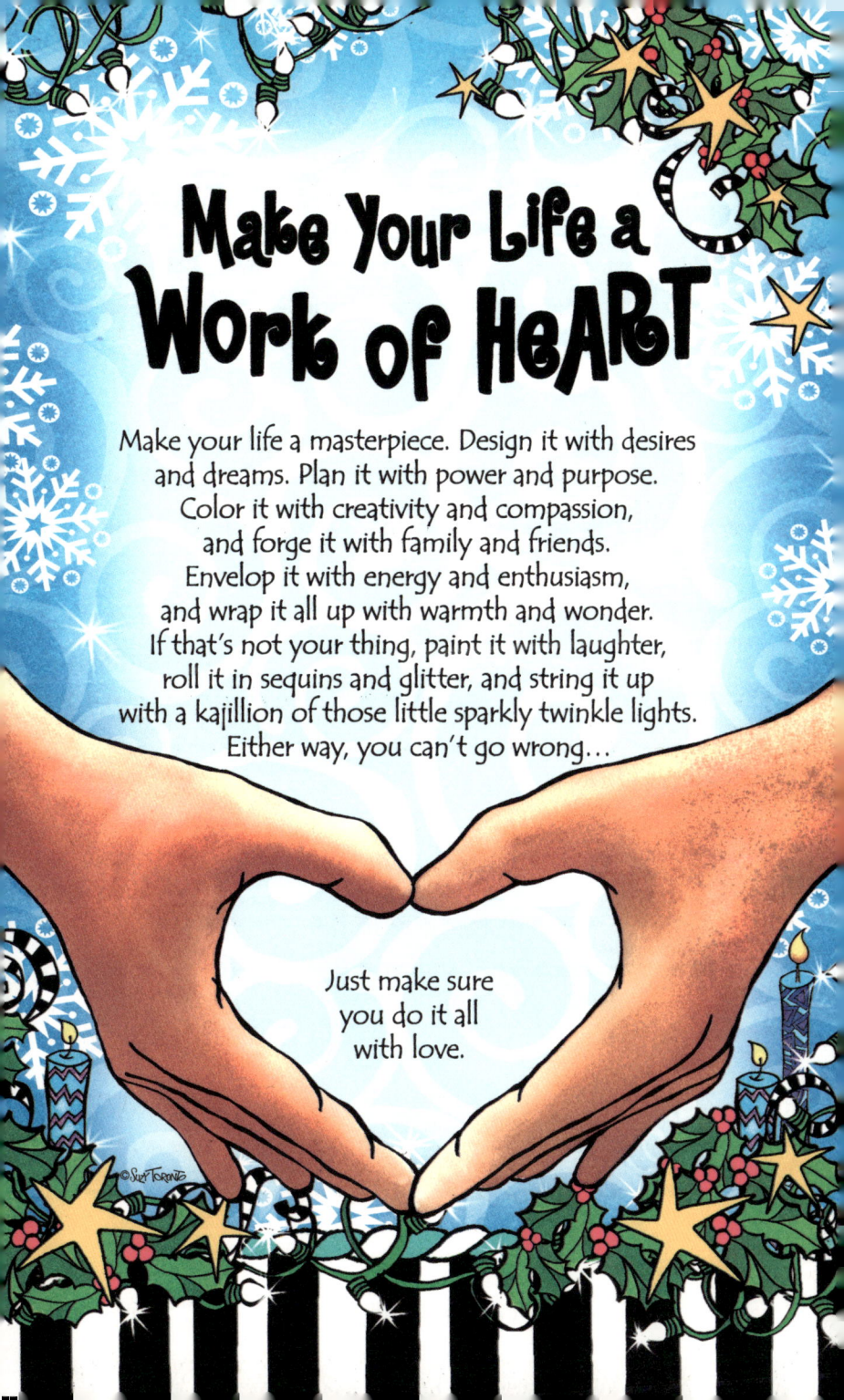

Make Your Life a Work of HeART

Make your life a masterpiece. Design it with desires
and dreams. Plan it with power and purpose.
Color it with creativity and compassion,
and forge it with family and friends.
Envelop it with energy and enthusiasm,
and wrap it all up with warmth and wonder.
If that's not your thing, paint it with laughter,
roll it in sequins and glitter, and string it up
with a kajillion of those little sparkly twinkle lights.
Either way, you can't go wrong...

Just make sure
you do it all
with love.

Always lead with your heart.
It's the best compass you've got.

Sunday, December 13

Monday, December 14

Tuesday, December 15

Wednesday, December 16

National Chocolate-Covered Anything Day
Day of Reconciliation (South Africa)

Thursday, December 17

Friday, December 18

Saturday, December 19

Notes:

The secret to happiness is to find joy in everything you do.

Sunday, December 20

Monday, December 21

Winter Begins

Tuesday, December 22

Wednesday, December 23

Thursday, December 24

Christmas Eve

Friday, December 25

Christmas

Saturday, December 26

First Day of Kwanzaa (USA)
Boxing Day (Canada/UK/Australia)
St. Stephen's Day (Ireland)
Day of Goodwill (South Africa)

In a World Where
Bigger
Is Always Better...
Think Small!

Sometimes we all think big way too much. Don't get me wrong — thinking up really big, wild, and crazy ideas is one of my favorite things to do. But life is also about finding the simple things that take our breath away and illuminate our tiny corner of the world. These tender moments give our lives deeper meaning and sometimes become our most treasured memories. Quite simply... they make our hearts tingle. It's moments like nuzzling a newborn baby's cheek and vowing never to forget that sweet smell. Or sitting on a porch swing with your grandmother and praying you'll always remember her voice. It's laughing at a silly joke between friends and hearing the echo of your own childhood giggles. It's waking up in the morning and really feeling grateful for one more day.

It's easy to get caught up in the rapture of life's brilliant, amazing, and spectacular things. But in the end, we must always remember that life is really no big thing... it's a zillion little things, just waiting to be cherished. Now take a deep breath... and feel the tingle!

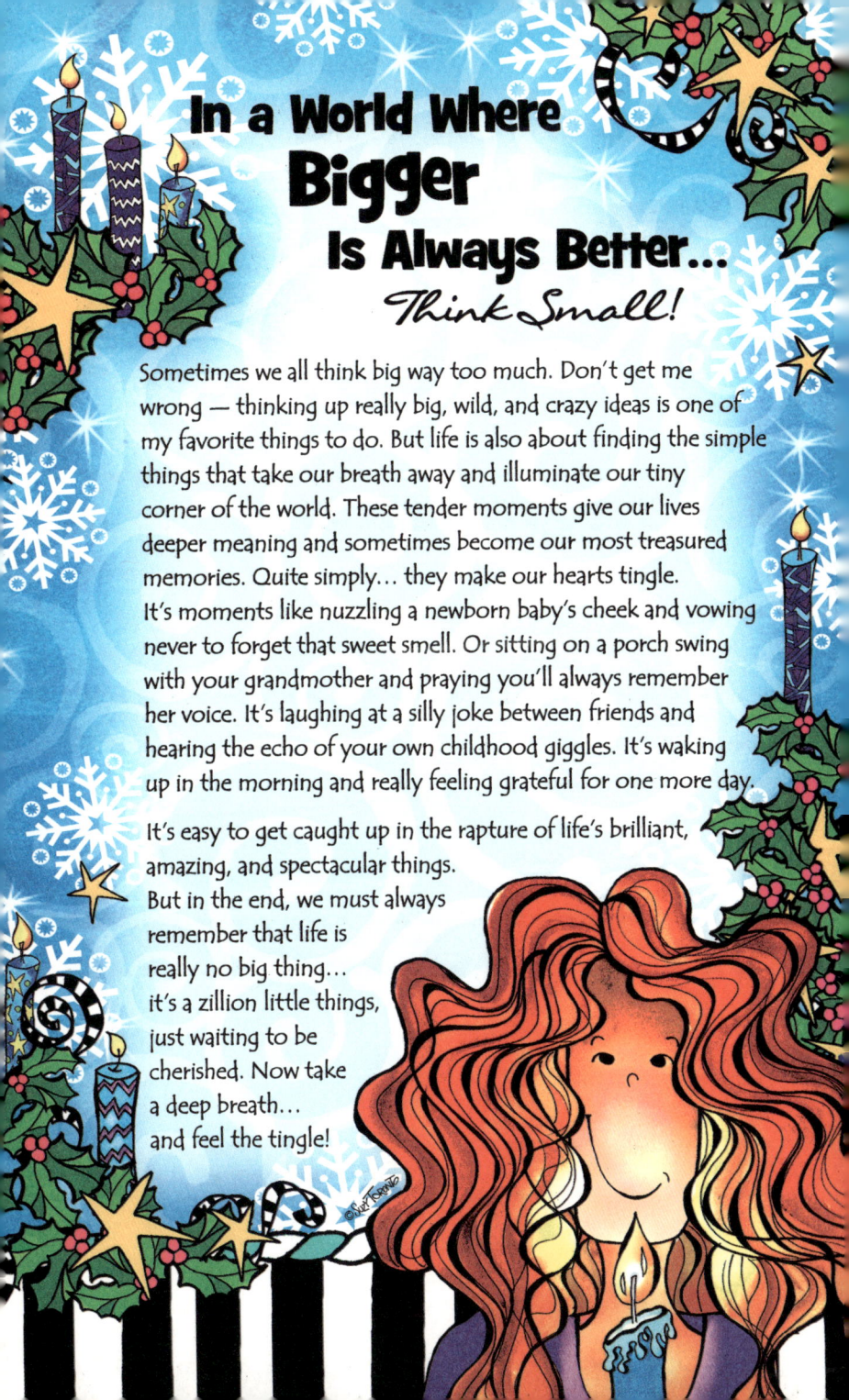

You are an eternal being of infinite worth.

Sunday, December 27

Monday, December 28

Bank Holiday (UK)
St. Stephen's Day Observed (Ireland)

Tuesday, December 29

Full Moon ◯

Wednesday, December 30

Thursday, December 31

New Year's Eve

Friday, January 1, 2021

New Year's Day

Saturday, January 2, 2021

Bank Holiday (Scotland)

Notes:

You are capable of far more than you've ever imagined. And you are limitless in every way.

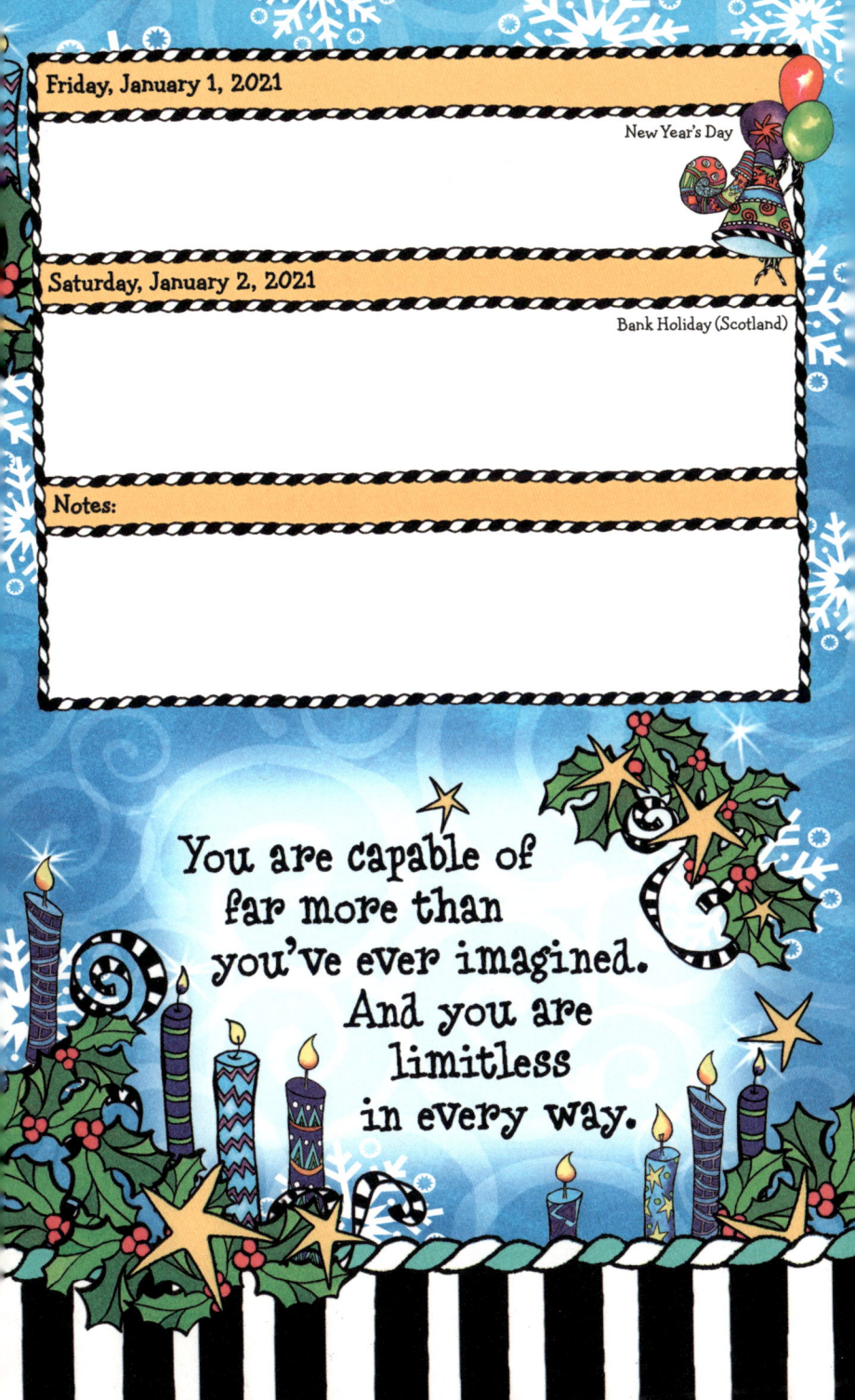

Important Stuff
Critical to My Life

Important Stuff
Critical to My Life

Mindless Stuff
Floating Around in My Head

Mindless Stuff
Floating Around in My Head

2020

The future's so bright, you gotta wear shades.

January
```
S  M  T  W  T  F  S
         1  2  3  4
5  6  7  8  9 10 11
12 13 14 15 16 17 18
19 20 21 22 23 24 25
26 27 28 29 30 31
```

February
```
S  M  T  W  T  F  S
                  1
2  3  4  5  6  7  8
9 10 11 12 13 14 15
16 17 18 19 20 21 22
23 24 25 26 27 28 29
```

March
```
S  M  T  W  T  F  S
1  2  3  4  5  6  7
8  9 10 11 12 13 14
15 16 17 18 19 20 21
22 23 24 25 26 27 28
29 30 31
```

April
```
S  M  T  W  T  F  S
         1  2  3  4
5  6  7  8  9 10 11
12 13 14 15 16 17 18
19 20 21 22 23 24 25
26 27 28 29 30
```

May
```
S  M  T  W  T  F  S
               1  2
3  4  5  6  7  8  9
10 11 12 13 14 15 16
17 18 19 20 21 22 23
24/31 25 26 27 28 29 30
```

June
```
S  M  T  W  T  F  S
   1  2  3  4  5  6
7  8  9 10 11 12 13
14 15 16 17 18 19 20
21 22 23 24 25 26 27
28 29 30
```

July
```
S  M  T  W  T  F  S
         1  2  3  4
5  6  7  8  9 10 11
12 13 14 15 16 17 18
19 20 21 22 23 24 25
26 27 28 29 30 31
```

August
```
S  M  T  W  T  F  S
                  1
2  3  4  5  6  7  8
9 10 11 12 13 14 15
16 17 18 19 20 21 22
23/30 24/31 25 26 27 28 29
```

September
```
S  M  T  W  T  F  S
      1  2  3  4  5
6  7  8  9 10 11 12
13 14 15 16 17 18 19
20 21 22 23 24 25 26
27 28 29 30
```

October
```
S  M  T  W  T  F  S
               1  2  3
4  5  6  7  8  9 10
11 12 13 14 15 16 17
18 19 20 21 22 23 24
25 26 27 28 29 30 31
```

November
```
S  M  T  W  T  F  S
1  2  3  4  5  6  7
8  9 10 11 12 13 14
15 16 17 18 19 20 21
22 23 24 25 26 27 28
29 30
```

December
```
S  M  T  W  T  F  S
      1  2  3  4  5
6  7  8  9 10 11 12
13 14 15 16 17 18 19
20 21 22 23 24 25 26
27 28 29 30 31
```

2021

Each year just keeps getting better & better.

January
```
S  M  T  W  T  F  S
                  1  2
3  4  5  6  7  8  9
10 11 12 13 14 15 16
17 18 19 20 21 22 23
24/31 25 26 27 28 29 30
```

February
```
S  M  T  W  T  F  S
   1  2  3  4  5  6
7  8  9 10 11 12 13
14 15 16 17 18 19 20
21 22 23 24 25 26 27
28
```

March
```
S  M  T  W  T  F  S
   1  2  3  4  5  6
7  8  9 10 11 12 13
14 15 16 17 18 19 20
21 22 23 24 25 26 27
28 29 30 31
```

April
```
S  M  T  W  T  F  S
               1  2  3
4  5  6  7  8  9 10
11 12 13 14 15 16 17
18 19 20 21 22 23 24
25 26 27 28 29 30
```

May
```
S  M  T  W  T  F  S
                  1
2  3  4  5  6  7  8
9 10 11 12 13 14 15
16 17 18 19 20 21 22
23/30 24/31 25 26 27 28 29
```

June
```
S  M  T  W  T  F  S
      1  2  3  4  5
6  7  8  9 10 11 12
13 14 15 16 17 18 19
20 21 22 23 24 25 26
27 28 29 30
```

July
```
S  M  T  W  T  F  S
               1  2  3
4  5  6  7  8  9 10
11 12 13 14 15 16 17
18 19 20 21 22 23 24
25 26 27 28 29 30 31
```

August
```
S  M  T  W  T  F  S
1  2  3  4  5  6  7
8  9 10 11 12 13 14
15 16 17 18 19 20 21
22 23 24 25 26 27 28
29 30 31
```

September
```
S  M  T  W  T  F  S
         1  2  3  4
5  6  7  8  9 10 11
12 13 14 15 16 17 18
19 20 21 22 23 24 25
26 27 28 29 30
```

October
```
S  M  T  W  T  F  S
                  1  2
3  4  5  6  7  8  9
10 11 12 13 14 15 16
17 18 19 20 21 22 23
24/31 25 26 27 28 29 30
```

November
```
S  M  T  W  T  F  S
   1  2  3  4  5  6
7  8  9 10 11 12 13
14 15 16 17 18 19 20
21 22 23 24 25 26 27
28 29 30
```

December
```
S  M  T  W  T  F  S
         1  2  3  4
5  6  7  8  9 10 11
12 13 14 15 16 17 18
19 20 21 22 23 24 25
26 27 28 29 30 31
```